My Kind of Crazy
Living in a Bipolar World

Cover image entitled Engel
© 2008 by Tyler Etzel Lyons
contact: Lyons2488@yahoo.com

Author's photo by Dana Dince

To order a symbolic purple bracelet
by Leaaron Designs
contact: ddince@mac.com

ISBN: 1-4392-1643-6
ISBN-13: 9781439216439
LCCN 2009900088

Visit www.booksurge.com to order additional copies.

My Kind of Crazy
Living in a Bipolar World

Janine Crowley Haynes

In loving memory of my mother

Kathleen Mary O'Keefe Crowley Young
(1943–1999)

Whose incredible strength, love, and wisdom
found a way to transcend linear time
and dwell in the realm of eternal presence.
You are my teacher of things great and small.
Your keen eye picked up on my hidden talents.
Your heart lovingly tended to bringing out that potential
and helped translate it into visual and verbal expression.
You have infused me with your sense of humor,
my secret weapon against adversity.
I'll meet you, as usual, in my dreams.
We'll have some coffee, and we'll talk.

To my husband, Larry,
Your silent strength is the Great Wall of our marriage.
At times, you have shielded me from myself.
I am forever grateful for your presence in my life.
You never cease to amaze me.

* * *

To my son, Steven,
You are my little warrior, a title unduly forced upon you.
When I attempted to take my life, you came to my rescue that dark night,
then found a way to soldier on.
You fought for your own sanity, licked your own wounds, and triumphed.
The greatest gift I have ever received in life is you, my sweet.

Acknowledgments

May all of my love and appreciation leap off this page and into the hearts of my family and friends. For over thirteen years now, you have witnessed this crazy roller coaster of manic swings and major depressions, yet never abandoned me. Rather, time and time again, you lovingly extended the drawbridge leading me back to sanity.

I would like to acknowledge my kind-hearted doctor, Anri Kissilenko. You are a gentle, gentle man who possesses wisdom and compassion to treat the patient as a whole. Thank you for never making me feel like a crazy person.

I would also like to thank the staff members of the Acute Care Unit at Silver Hill Hospital. There is no greater gift than giving of oneself for the sake of others. Your work can be tiresome, yet you are tireless. May each of you know that your care has meant a great deal to me. That being said, please don't take it personally when I say that I hope I never have to see any one of you ever again in a hospital setting. However, if I require another visit, I know I will be in good hands once more.

In addition, I would like to dedicate my story to those who happen to find themselves struggling with a mental illness. It is my heartfelt wish that my experience will offer some hope to you during the dark times. The added burden of being subjected to the stigma attached to mental illness is not only emotionally painful, but isolating as well. Hope can easily escape us all when we are at our most vulnerable, so never give up hope…never.

Table of Contents

What Crazy Looks Like/
What Crazy Feels Like

CHAPTER I

I am crazy. There—I said it. Crazy is a blanket term that covers all kinds of mental disorders. The medical term for my kind of crazy is *bipolar disorder*, aka *manic-depressive illness*. Now, I know it's not politically correct to use the word *crazy* when referring to anyone with a mental illness, but I wear the name like a badge of honor. I think I've earned it. I may not look crazy. In fact, I look quite normal. People are somewhat surprised when they find out and respond by saying, "But you don't look crazy." Most people laugh it off when someone calls them crazy. I laugh it off, too, knowing all too well that I can produce the certifiable papers to prove my craziness.

For some reason, the term *bipolar* sounds incredibly sophisticated. It makes me feel like I should possess a special talent or gift. To me, the word implies savant-like capabilities. The label *crazy* is equivalent to the GED of mental disorders, whereas *bipolar* sounds more like holding a PhD in the field. "Congratulations, you are bipolar! Here is your certificate." At the very least, the *bi* preceding the *polar* should enable me to do two different things at once.

An acquaintance once told me how lucky I was to be bipolar and that I should not be afraid of it, but rather embrace it. He went on to say that being bipolar was a gift from God. "Well, that's just crazy talk," I replied. I considered my condition more of a curse than a blessing. If you were to consult my husband or son on the matter, I'm sure they would agree with me. Although, I have to say, this somewhat stranger's words got me thinking.

To embrace this thing called bipolar disorder is not an easy task. You live day to day with the realization that you can lose your mind at any given moment. It's not my intention to minimize other physical ailments, because they are truly hardships as well. However, losing control of your sanity brings along with it a fear that can only be understood through the experience.

I am not alone with my mental illness. I am only one in 5.7 million adult Americans who are diagnosed with a mental illness in a given year. Within that figure, 2.6 percent are diagnosed with bipolar disorder.[1] As opposed to the psychoanalytical perspective of mental illness, the purpose of my story is to shed light on the human aspect of living with bipolar disorder. It's my hope that I can reach out to others with this condition. Whether it is a loved one or yourself who is affected by a mental illness, it can be a frightening ordeal.

---

[1] Statistics derived from The National Institute of Mental Health according to the 2004 U.S. Census.

Mind you, I am not an experienced, award-winning writer. My mixed metaphors and misplaced modifiers are testament to my virginal prose. In fact, this is my first attempt at writing. I'm not a celebrity who can use my illness as a platform. I'm not a doctor, nor do I recommend any one treatment. For the sake of authenticity, I acknowledge that certain parts of my story may be embellished due to being in a psychotic state where hallucinations tend to run wild. As far as I'm concerned, the real versus the unreal is an integral part of the illness and deserves equal recognition. Acknowledging every state of our being is what is pure and true.

Now that I've gotten all of the disclaimers out of the way, what I bring to you is my experience of living life as a crazy person.

After living with this disorder for over thirteen years, I struggle to find the right words to describe it. The bipolar experience has to do with going through extreme mood swings—from mania to depression, from anger and rage to paranoia, from apathy leading to eventual despair. There are as many different degrees and patterns of this disorder as there are bipolar individuals.

When I am in the beginning of the manic phase, it's like looking at the ocean during high tide on a bright sunny day. Standing at the edge of the sand where the vast ocean meets my insignificant self, I watch the waves come crashing in all around me, one after the other. It excites and exhilarates me. My senses become heightened. The flow of the ocean brings along with it all sorts of possibilities. My creative energies soar; I feel like I can do anything. This high can last for days, weeks, or even months. Eating and sleeping are just an afterthought.

Then all at once, a million thoughts come rushing in. I can't keep up. Soon my thoughts become scattered. Eventually, the feeling of invincibility deteriorates into vulnerability. A perpetual tremor radiates through my extremities. Suddenly, I am engulfed by an enormous wave, and I am dragged out to sea by a riptide. Now, miles away from solid ground, I fight fiercely against the current. Panic sets in as I struggle to stay afloat. My heart is racing. As I gasp for air, salt water fills my lungs. I fight against the current, but something reminds me not to fight. If I allow the current to take me out farther, then it will release me. *Tread water, stay afloat,* I tell myself, but I'm terrified and tired. I begin to sink. For a moment, I let go of control. The surreal sense of it all overwhelms me, but then I choose to fight. Finally, another wave comes along, and the ocean spits me back onto the shore like some bad shellfish that it had for lunch. As I lie in the sand, I gaze at the sky. It turns from blue to gray. The ocean quiets and the shore begins to recede. The low tide of depression sets in. Then I become paralyzed by feelings of hopelessness and despair.

My first official breakdown happened over thirteen years ago, just one month after my thirtieth birthday. Since then, I've repeatedly experienced this relentless bipolar cycle. Along with each episode comes a new twist. The last time I was caught in the riptide, I surrendered. I sank to a new depth. In less flowery words, I swallowed a bunch of pills to put myself out of the never-ending misery. I even went as far as to convince myself that my family would be better off without the burden of my illness. Contrary to what Shakespeare might have us believe, there is nothing noble, poetic, or lyrical about suicide. Please forgive me for not being able to express my remorse. Suffice it to say, I want to kill myself for trying to kill myself.

The regrets I have pale in comparison to the pain I have caused my husband, son, extended family, and friends. I will never forgive myself for inflicting such a trauma on my loved ones. Although I know my son loves me, the hurt and fear that remains in his blue eyes pierces like a dagger straight through to my soul. Understandably, his trust in me has been broken, and the damage—irreparable. Telling my family that I'm sorry just doesn't cut it. My doctors readily justify my suicide attempt as being part of the nature of the illness and say I should not be held accountable for my actions, just as I cannot be held responsible when I am psychotic and believe that I am Mother Nature. Somehow, I can accept not being personally responsible for droughts or tsunamis, but I am solely responsible for my suicide attempt. I can't use my illness as an excuse.

Over the years, I have had numerous hospital stays, various doctors, countless therapy sessions, and a wide array of medication regimens. During my committals, I have met all kinds of people with different mental afflictions and alcohol and drug addictions. For some people, it can be a three-in-one combination.

Not to get all Confucius on you, but my mother tried to instill in me the belief that there is a lesson to be learned from every experience we encounter. The challenge is to find the lesson, learn from it, and then pass on that wisdom. It's easier said than done, but I truly want to believe that it is possible.

I can't help but wonder why this bipolar cycle continues to repeat itself. Is it because I am just not *getting it*, or am I supposed to be honing my endurance and long-suffering techniques? Could it be that the lesson to be learned here is that there is no lesson at all—*it* just is what *it* is? If that's so, maybe I can learn to accept it and find the peace I so desire. For me, finding this peace of mind is like discovering the Holy Grail in a landfill after spending a lifetime sifting through all of the debris. They say that the devil is in the details, or is it God that's in the details? I can't remember. Anyway, what they don't tell you is that looking for *it* can drive you crazy. And, if or when you finally do find *it*, well wouldn't you know, *it* was right there in front of you all along.

Incognito

CHAPTER II

I like to paint my face and put on my sunglasses so I can go outside. Somehow the facade of makeup and the anonymity of sunglasses act as a shield that keeps me from exposing my real self. I wonder if other people feel the same way. I miss that feeling when I check into the spa. Well, to be honest, it's not a spa—it's a psychiatric hospital that I tend to frequent on a routine basis. Over the past thirteen years, my visits average out to be at least once a year (sometimes more) for a minimum stay of two weeks and a maximum stay of five weeks.

When I check into the hospital, my naked self is exposed for all to see. A body scan is what they call it. I am stripped of all things; mostly my pride. They also take away anything sharp I could cut myself with and any items that can be used to constrict, constrain, or hang myself with. Among these items are keys, razors, makeup compacts that have mirrors in them, belts, and shoelaces, just to name a few. You can always tell who's on suicide watch by the absence of laces in their shoes or sneakers.

* * *

Once again, I am admitted to the psych ward. A suicide attempt is a sure way to get oneself committed. As I am being strip-searched, I regret not packing a bag in advance. These hospital visits are routine; I should know better. This leaves me subject to my husband's practical yet tasteless packing skills, which tend to lack style and variety—but he never forgets to pack my snowflake pajamas. This visit, I'm determined to be more assertive. I will attempt to use my seniority and strongly request one of the more private rooms at the far end of the hall. They are more desirable since they're farther away from the hustle and flow of migratory patients rushing back and forth to the public areas. While a couple of the staff members rifle through my belongings, I make it clear that I want a private room at the end of the hall. They humor me and say that although the unit is fully booked, they'll put me on the waiting list. I could swear I saw one of them rolling their eyes at me, but it could very well be one of my hallucinations. I've learned not to trust myself in that way.

One of the health technicians escorts me to my room. Damn it, the room is right outside the Fishbowl—command central of the Acute Care Unit (ACU). It's this glass-enclosed circular structure where the staff is stationed and on display for the patients to poke fun at. Needless to say, it's a noisy location. There's always some patient banging on the glass, declaring his seventy-two-hour notice of release. No matter how delusional patients may be, they always seem to be cognizant enough to know their legal rights.

As the health tech brings me to my room, I am faced with another surprise—a roommate. There is no introduction since she is engrossed in making a drawing consisting solely of a million little dots.

"So, would you like a tour of the unit?" the tech asks me.

"You must be new here," I comment. "I've accumulated a lifetime of frequent-flyer miles, enough to cover this flight to hell and back again. Please make sure the administration applies those miles to my bill, and I don't want to hear that this week is blacked out."

"Well, alrighty then...in that case, my name is Christie, and I'll be your flight attendant for the rest of the day. Make sure your seat and tray are in the upright position, and please don't hesitate to push the button if you are in need of assistance." She smiles as she leaves the room, then pops her head back in and says, "Oh, just so you know, there's a group session in the Day Room in about forty-five minutes."

The ability to go with the ebb and flow of a patient is a must for someone in her position. I think we may very well get along. Health techs are equivalent to soldiers on the frontline. They are the ones on foot patrol overseeing the patients and keeping order.

The Day Room functions for a multitude of activities. It's where all the group sessions take place and where meals are served. At night, it turns into a TV and game room. One of the most desirable features of the Day Room is that it holds the only doorway leading to the outdoor deck, which is made up of concrete slabs with a few park-like benches, and surrounded by panels of wire mesh screening about nine feet high designed to ward off escape. There's nothing to hold onto, making it impossible to scale. The deck does, however, allow patients to escape the stale air of the institution in exchange for some fresh air mixed with cigarette smoke. We all watch and wait for that precious deck time, which comes along every couple of hours in ten to fifteen minute increments.

There's another room on the other side of the Fishbowl called the Music Room, which is a dual-purpose room. This room contains a stereo, television, and either a VCR or DVD. At night, patients can reserve the Music Room in advance, and only four or five people are permitted to use it at one time. Some mornings, the Music Room serves as the recovery room for patients undergoing shock treatment, aka, electroconvulsive therapy (ECT).

The ACU is a locked unit and has approximately thirteen private rooms and two semi-private rooms for patients. There are also two other "special rooms." One is for the incredibly incapacitated patient. It looks like a typical hospital room—stark, no carpeting, etc. The other room is for the completely out-of-control patient (temporary solitary confinement). That room is called the Quiet Room. No one ever wants to go the Quiet Room. I'm not sure why it's called the Quiet Room. Its name makes it sound like a serene refuge where one could go to meditate or maybe even do some Tai Chi. All I know is that whenever I've had occasion to visit the Quiet Room, it was anything but quiet. I guess the thick cinder block walls help to soundproof and insulate the room to afford quietude, not for the Quiet Room, but for the rest of the ward. The room is completely empty except for an old torn gym mat from the seventies that rests upon the painted gray cement floor. Surprisingly, there's no padding on the walls to provide extra comfort in case someone decides to incessantly slam his or her head against it. At least they're civil enough not to put you in a straight jacket. Now that would be barbaric.

Aside from the medication closet, where we line up for happy hour and drink our medicinal cocktails, that concludes the tour of the ACU. Over time, as a patient gets better, he or she can move to another house on the hospital campus for further recovery. One house is for continued recovery from a mental illness; another house is for helping those with alcohol and drug dependencies. There's also a house for transitional living for those getting ready to go back out into the world. These environments are much more conducive to the healing process. There is more freedom. Although these other houses on the hospital campus have rules, their best feature is that there are no fences or locked doors like the ACU. They are considered to be the "open" facilities, whereas the ACU is the "closed" facility.

Please don't be mistaken. I happen to be one of the lucky ones to be admitted to Silver Hill, a private psychiatric hospital, situated in a beautiful bucolic setting amongst one of the more affluent communities in Connecticut. The prices of the homes in this area start at a million and go up from there. I wonder, though, if that's the case for the houses surrounding the hospital. From time to time, the occasional breakout occurs, and a patient is found meandering about on a neighboring property. That's gotta bring the prices down just a little bit. Don't ya think?

Sometimes patients elope. This is when two patients work as a tag team and attempt to flee the ACU when authorized personnel enter or exit the locked facility. I was not familiar with this term during a previous visit when a patient asked me to elope. Even though I was flattered, I told him that I hardly knew him. I went on to explain that my responsibilities as Mother Nature took up way too much of my time to be involved in a serious relationship. Being Mother Nature does not allow for such folly; I was busy controlling weather patterns, gravitational pull, etc. My suitor raised one eyebrow and, with complete understanding, replied, "I hear ya—nuff said." He didn't take it personally. He just moved on to his next prospect.

Time passes while I reminisce on such good times. My meager belongings have already been placed on my bed to be put away. I peruse the room and try to make peace with the all-too-familiar surroundings, speculating how long this visit will last. I decide to introduce myself to my roommate, who is still dotting away.

I walk over to her side of the room and say, "Hi, I'm Janine."

She makes no eye contact and mumbles, "Tess."

The absence of a follow up question leads to the presence of an awkward pause and prompts me to return my side of the room. As I put away my clothes, an announcement comes over the loudspeaker: "Group is starting in the Day Room. All patients are expected to attend."

"Tess, are you going to group?" I ask.

She barely looks up from her pointillist creation. "My work here is far more important than any group session."

I think to myself, *Wow, what conviction—a true artist!*

"Oh and I think it would be best if you make yourself scarce. Your presence here is a distraction," she adds while dismissing me with her hand.

"Uh, uh, I'll see what I can do," I meekly reply and scurry out the door.

On my way to the Day Room, I'm greeted by a few familiar faces. They are the faces of the nurses and health technicians who have taken care of me in the past. It's always nice to be recognized, but being famous among the staff of a psych ward, I'm thinking, is maybe not so nice.

Debbie, one of my favorite techs, yells out, "Hey, Janine! What are you doing back so soon?" We violate the "no contact rule" and hug.

"Sometimes even Mother Nature needs a rest." I wink jokingly, wondering if she remembers my last psychotic episode when I believed I controlled weather patterns and things of that nature.

"Say no more; I hope that you get a good rest." She gets me.

As I enter the Day Room for group, all eyes turn to me. The group circle has already been formed with no available seating. Chad, one of the therapists, is conducting the session. He recognizes me and says, "Welcome, old friend. Pull up a chair." The circle parts just enough for me to squeeze in, and the old woman sitting next to me gives me the handout entitled "How to Take Control of Your Illness."

As the session moves along, the voices around me become muffled; my attention turns to the faces in the circle. Crazy comes in all colors, shapes, and sizes. Crazy does not discriminate. Let me see now; sitting around the circle are a male, female, male, female, female, male, female—no maybe male. I'm not quite sure. There are two blondes, four brunettes, and one slightly bald with gray mixed in. Crazy comes fat and sometimes even fatter. Crazy comes skinny and sometimes really, really skinny. Some of them look like they once were *somebody*. Some look like they never even had a chance to be *somebody*. Some are fidgeting with their hands, others are tapping their toes, and one is picking his nose. Some are tearing up and filled with emotion, like the old woman next to me, while others are frozen in a drug-induced, slack-jawed stupor.

Please understand, I make no judgments, only observations. For I am one of them.

Margaret

CHAPTER III

The group session ends and patients disperse. I remain seated, pretending to read the handout. My vision is blurred—a common side effect brought on by the heavy dosage of antipsychotic medication running through my bloodstream. The old woman sitting beside me reaches out and latches onto my arm in an attempt to heave herself up from the chair, only to fall back down. She looks to be in her late seventies. Her frail body shakes with tremors that sometimes accompany certain medications. She continues to sob the way she did throughout the entire session.

"Are you okay?" I ask, making a halfhearted attempt to show some compassion.

"He's going to leave me! I know he is. What I am going to do? Oh God, I just want to die." She continues to wail. "He doesn't love me anymore. I know he doesn't. That harlot! She's going to steal him away. I knew I couldn't trust her when she moved in. She did this. They did this together. They put me here so they can run away together." She leans in, grabs me with her claw-like hand, and whispers, "When I accused my husband of sleeping with my sister, he said I was crazy. Next thing I know, I end up here." The desperation shows in her face. "Please help me. I beg you, help me, please."

"I could get you some water. Will that help? Would you like some water?" I ask, not knowing what else to do for her.

"No, no," she wails. "I *need* help. I need to win him back. He's coming to visit me tonight."

Just when I think she's about to draw me into some kind of scheme, she looks at me with the vulnerability of an insecure teenage girl, bows her head shyly, and softly whispers, "I need to look pretty for him when he comes later. Do you have makeup? You look like you would have makeup. Can you make me pretty?"

Her plea melts my heart. "What's your name?"

"Margaret."

"Well, Margaret, let's get busy. I'll meet you in your room."

I return to my room to get what little makeup they let me keep when I checked in. Since I neglected to ask Margaret which room she is in, I endure the dirty looks from other patients as I poke my head into each room along the hallway until I see her. It figures, Margaret occupies one of the coveted rooms at the end of the hall. Although I'm not supposed to enter her room, I do anyway. She's sitting on the edge of her bed, waiting for me. The curtains are drawn and the room is dark. I pull back the curtain, allowing the setting sun to cast a soft amber light on her face. I hesitate for a moment as I study the weathered lines on her face. Why do we feel the need to erase our wrinkles?

They define who we are and tell our stories. On second thought, maybe that's why we feel so compelled.

I apply a little eye shadow to her sagging lids, dust some blush onto her hollow cheekbones, and dab some gloss onto her shriveled lips. I brush out her matted, over-processed blonde hair and sweep it back away from her face.

Pleased with my efforts, I smile and say, "Okay, Margaret, you're all set."

She slowly makes her way to the bathroom and leans in just an inch away from the non-breakable mirror, which tends to distort your image. As she peers into the mirror, she runs her fingers over her face and smiles at herself. "Now I'm pretty. Now he'll have to love me again."

My heart breaks for Margaret. I thoroughly understand the pain of rejection. Being in a mental institution is enough to make you feel rejected from society, but to have your husband check you into a psych ward in order to run away with your sister has got to make you feel worse, even if you're in your late seventies.

The Raven and the Turtle

CHAPTER IV

After leaving Margaret's room, I return to the Day Room since Tess has made it quite clear that she doesn't welcome my company. Fussing with a Rubik's Cube helps to pass the time, but doesn't the staff realize this cube only leads us crazies to further madness? I toss the damn thing into the trash.

People rush in for the evening slop. Dinner is being put out on the buffet table in individual Styrofoam cartons, each labeled with a patient's first name and last initial. I open mine and shrink back as I attempt to identify which food group it might belong to. Suddenly, the week-old egg foo young I left in my fridge doesn't sound half bad. I leave it on the table and move just a few feet away from the dining area to the television area. I notice my favorite seat in the corner near the television is available.

Having my possessions taken away leaves a void, which instinctively needs to be filled with something. Right now, that chair is mine. Trying not to be obvious, I move swiftly yet deliberately to stake my claim, and then curl up in a fetal position. It's freezing in here. No matter what season it is, it's always freezing in the ACU. I wrap my sweater even more tightly around me and pull my hood over my head, hoping to get an extra blanket tonight, maybe even an extra pillow. My mind zones out as I fix my gaze on the TV. Feelings of guilt begin to creep into my mind about my suicide attempt. *How did I let myself get so far out of control?* Over the years, I've prided myself on being able to identify when I was slipping. Just as I begin to bathe myself in guilt, someone interrupts.

"Hey, you're the new girl, right?" he asks.

"I am," I reply with the hope that he'll go away and leave me to my thoughts.

"Are you going to eat your meal?"

"No. You can have it," I say, relieved that my food is all he wants.

"Thanks. Don't worry. I won't tell the staff that you didn't eat your dinner."

"I appreciate that. And, don't you worry…I won't tell the staff that you pick your nose and eat it. I guess you're really hungry."

He giggles nervously as he walks away.

After dinner and dessert are served, we wait for the deck to be opened. We all huddle around the door until the gate master opens it up. A rush of crisp, cold air strikes my face and wakes me up. I'm so grateful that Petey is on duty. He is one of the most compassionate health techs on the unit. He has long, light brown hair, hippy clothing, and a heart of gold. He kind of reminds me of John Corbett's character, Chris Stevens, from *Northern Exposure*.

Petey never fails to bring his guitar to entertain us. First and foremost, though, he hands out the cigarettes to those who smoke, each from a separate envelope marked with the person's name. He is the sole keeper of the one and only lighter, with which he lights cigarette after cigarette, asking each individual, "Hey, what's up?" Everyone feels comfortable with him. Petey has a certain, special something—he can always calm down a patient on a rant.

Once everyone is set with their cigarettes, tiny cliques form. A few sit ostracized around the perimeter. Some of us crowd around Petey when he begins to play. He also takes requests. I sit on the bench next to him as he plays my usual request, "Landslide." A few people sing the lyrics while I sit with my eyes closed imagining I'm making angels in the snow. We all shake and shiver from the cold, but no one dares to go back in. Our deck time is too precious and fleeting to prematurely return to the inside. Soon enough, we will retreat. We always retreat.

"What are you in for?" a young woman asks. Her elongated physique towers over me as she waits for my reply. My eyes scale this lengthy figure—her feet tucked into a pair of Uggs; her body shrouded in a woven poncho; her hair long, black, straight, and silky; her complexion taut, smooth, and caramel-colored; her eyes shiny black onyxes.

"For trying to kill myself," I reply, not believing the words as they come out of my mouth. Before she can reply, I shoot back, "What about you? What are you in for?"

Without hesitation, she reveals, "ED and alcohol and drugs."

ED is short for *eating disorder*. It's hard to believe she could have anything wrong with her when she looks so picture perfect. The thing about people with ED is that they have become masters at covering it up. Later in the conversation, I find out this woman is part Native American, a descendant of the Crow tribe. Here in the unit, she goes by her Indian name, Raven. She also reveals to me that she's a runway model. Some patients decide not to use their real names for the sake of anonymity.

As we make our way back inside, I comment, "Raven—that's such a cool name."

She smiles and asks, "Would you like to walk the Circle with me?"

"Sure."

The Circle is the walk that patients take down the hallway, around the Fishbowl, down the other hallway, and back again. As we walk, the Raven further enlightens me. "The raven is part of the crow family and is said to be the most intelligent amongst all birds. They can even learn to speak. In some Native American tribes, it's believed that they possess creative and mystical powers."

"Wow, I didn't know that."

"We are now at the end of the winter season, which is when the raven is truly in her element. Her powers and creativity are heightened." Raven speaks with such intrigue. "Winter solstice, which marks the shortest and darkest day of the year, has passed. After that, the days get lighter and lighter. That's why I decided to check into the hospital now. I'll have a better chance of recovery."

"What do you mean?" I ask her in the way a student would ask a teacher.

"Like the raven, one must know the darkness first and then find the creative energy to turn the darkness back into light."

I step back and try to absorb this wisdom, but she continues.

"Have any animals crossed your path lately—maybe in your dreams?"

I think for a moment. "Strangely enough, yes: a turtle. I don't remember all the details of the dream, but I remember that the turtle was upside down and half-eaten. It was struggling to turn itself over."

"Ah, in some native tribes, the turtle is the symbol of Mother Earth."

"Hmm, that's interesting." Now I start to wonder whether or not she's mocking me. How does she know of my previous occupation?

"If you have a turtle in your totem, it should remind you that Mother Earth provides for all of our needs. What people forget is that we must care for Her in return. It looks like the turtle in your dream has been damaged and is fighting to save itself. The turtle means that you should slow down. Go within your shell. Take the time to think and to heal. Don't come out of your shell until you've given enough thought to what your next move will be."

"Okay," I say skeptically. "That's good to know."

The Raven draws back her hair to reveal two black feathers intertwined in her black mane near the nape of her neck. She pulls one of the feathers out and weaves it into my hair. "This will help to cleanse your spirit and get rid of any negative energy, which will enable you to heal."

"I don't know what to say. That's pretty deep. Thanks, but how do you know about these things?"

"Knowledge is the nature of the raven. However, the struggle of the raven is that it possesses the knowledge but not always the wisdom. The raven can learn to speak but does not always know what it is saying." Then she adds, "Oh yeah, I also read it in a book. By the way, I never asked your name."

I hesitate for a second and then confess, "Around here, I go by the name of Mother Nature."

She raises one eyebrow as we share an *ah-ha* moment, and with complete understanding, the Raven flies away.

Happy Hour

CHAPTER V

An announcement comes over the speaker: "Good evening, ladies and gentlemen, the time is now 10 p.m. It's time to come and get your meds. Get your meds here! Thank you, and have a good night and pleasant tomorrow." Petey always adds a personal touch to the announcements.

A line has already formed by the med closet. The door to the med closet is one of those Dutch doors that open up on top while the bottom remains closed and has a little shelf to rest the medications—sort of like the back door in *Green Acres*. Everyone has a different ritual when it comes to taking meds. Some swallow a whole bunch of pills at once, while others slowly take one pill at a time. Others demand to know the name of each pill and what it's for. Some refuse to take any meds at all.

As I wait in line, I exchange pleasantries with a fellow patient standing behind me.

"Fuck you, you blonde-haired bitch."

I look around to realize that I am the only blonde-haired bitch in line.

"Huh? What did I do?" I ask.

"You cut the line."

"Oh, I'm sorry, I didn't realize. By all means, you can go before me."

She slips in front of me and proceeds to berate the guy in front of her.

"Fuck you, you blue-eyed bastard."

And that's how she makes her way to the head of the line. My turn at the med window eventually comes.

"Hey, Carol," I say to the medication nurse.

"Janine, what are you doing back so soon?"

I can tell she is genuinely concerned and sad to see me.

Too exhausted to explain, I ignore her question as she hands me a Dixie cup filled with a personalized medicinal concoction.

"Tonight, Carol, I'm in a one-shot kind of mood."

Like one would do with a tequila shot, I jerk my head back and take a big swig, washing all the pills down.

"Where's the lime to bite down on?"

Carol smiles and says in a maternal voice, "Sleep good, sweetie."

After the meds kick in, the real therapy sessions take place. The night divulges a multitude of secrets. Truth serum comes in many forms; usually in the form of a heavy dosage of anti-psychotic, anti-anxiety, or sleep medication. The curtain on the stage is drawn back, and the show commences forthwith. Like in a circus act, individual spotlights shine on each of us, yet we all perform in tandem. The vapor of inhibition leaves our bodies and hovers slightly above us as we take to the stage. We tend to unload all of the shit that we feel too ashamed to address in the group sessions. Tonight, a girl named Marla explains to me the reasons why she cuts herself.

"My stepfather molested me when I was eleven years old."

"Oh, that's terrible. Did your mother know?"

"Yeah, I told her, but she didn't really believe me. She was so fuckin' afraid of losing him. The perv ended up leaving her after I spoke up."

"It's a good thing you said something."

"Well, it's not like he raped me. He just felt me up every now and then. I guess I should consider myself lucky. My mom is more messed up over the whole thing than I am. She's been medicated for over ten years."

"I am so sorry, Marla."

She shrugs. "No worries. That's why I cut myself. It's the way I get relief, but nobody seems to get that—not even my mother."

During the course of our conversation, Marla repeatedly slices into her wrist with her shortened thumbnail, which makes it difficult to penetrate the surface of her skin. I suspect the staff trimmed down her natural weapons upon admission, but that does not deter her—cutters are incredibly persistent. By the end of our conversation, Marla manages to break skin, only to leave yet another scar to dwell amongst the countless others.

The duration of this circus act never lasts long. The performers are weary from the final impact of the meds. Our palates become parched. We begin to slur our words and walk in a zombie-like motion back to our rooms. The velvet curtain unfurls. There are no curtain calls. There are no encores.

From the exhaustion of the day, I stagger back to my room. Tess is still dotting away. I pull on my green flannel pajamas with the large white snowflakes on them. I always insist that my husband pack them for my hospital visits because they keep me warm and, of course, because they have snowflakes on them. Then I collapse onto the rigid bed. No one in my family knows that I pray every night before I go to sleep. I don't pray in the conventional way. I don't kneel. I don't make the sign of the cross or recite any Our Fathers or Hail Marys. It's more of a running dialogue between the powers that be and little old me. My gratitude for being spared humbles me, but my guilt for attempting to take my life consumes me. I pray for divine healing for my son and to ease the pain I have caused him. I pray that he heals from the trauma that I inflicted upon him. A twelve-year-old boy should never be witness to such a horrific fiasco. It is my hope, my prayer, that in the long run he will be okay. I hope something positive can come from my hideous act and that he becomes a stronger person because of it. I pray for his forgiveness, but it seems impossible.

I don't remember all of the details from the night of my suicide attempt, except that my husband and son went for pizza and then to his basketball game without me. I chose to stay at home brooding over the realization that I was sick again. Resolved in belief that I would never recover, fear ripped through me. It was too much to bear. I wanted the cycle of torment to end once and for all. There was no premeditation. I didn't plan my suicide for days, weeks, or months in advance. It was a rash decision made by an irrational, sick brain.

I spilled a bunch of different pills onto the kitchen counter, ran the faucet, filled a glass, and gulped the battery of pills down without considering how it would affect my family. After I swallowed them, I remember going upstairs to dress in something that would be appropriate for my funeral. Naturally, I put on a fresh pair of underwear, which my grandmother always told me I should have on just in case I died unexpectedly. Then whoever found me could say, "Well, at least she had on clean underwear." I proceeded to put on a formal black pantsuit with a sheer blouse that had a black ribbon embroidered on it. It revealed my breasts since I didn't bother to search for a camisole. I don't remember if I ever put on a pair of shoes to complete the ensemble. After I finished dressing, I removed the black comforter from my bed and placed it in the bathtub; I thought the tub was a fitting coffin. Then I locked the bathroom door behind me, but not before I wrote a thoughtful suicide note, which I taped to the front of the bathroom door so as to warn my husband before entering. How considerate of me.

How selfish I am. How stupid I am. I hate myself. I hate myself. I hate myself.

My thoughts return to my present predicament. I lie in my hospital bed staring at the wall, and the silent cry ensues. We all know that cry, the salty tears that run down your face, but there is no energy to make even the slightest sound. The silent tears are the only external sign of release. It's the kind of cry where your heart hurts, your throat closes, and the pain coursing through your veins funnels out to your extremities and back again. The feeling is all too familiar. I wish I could kiss my husband and son goodnight. I pray for their forgiveness most of all. There is nothing I wouldn't do to make amends for my transgressions.

Mercifully, the medications take over and send me drifting off to sleep as I watch the Raven fly over the Turtle.

Steven

CHAPTER VI

While I slumber in my hospital bed, I want to jump briefly ahead to give you another perspective of "the incident." It is the perspective of my son, Steven. Just about a year after my suicide attempt, I began writing about the experience. I wasn't planning to share my writings with anyone—let alone with my husband or son—but one day Steven leaned over me while I was typing on the computer. He saw the word *crazy* woven into the paragraph. With worry in his eyes, he asked me, "Mom, what's this about?"

At that point, I had no other choice but to be honest with him. Knowing that he is a writer at heart, I attempted to sound intellectual about an emotional subject by saying, "I'm journaling about my bipolar disorder."

Since he was a little boy, he's loved to write. He started out writing short stories and poetry. Now that he's older, his stories have grown into mature, descriptive tales, and his poetry is quite lyrical.

Once I explained what I was doing, Steven mustered up the courage to ask me what happened the night of the incident.

"Mom, why did you try to kill yourself?"

I struggled to find the right words to explain the logic of my madness.

"I was desperate to relieve my pain. I was scared, and I didn't want to go back to the hospital. I thought that you and Dad would be better off without me and my illness."

He looked at me with sad eyes and said, "Well, in the future, if you ever feel that way again, just know that it's not true. We need you, Mom."

His words humbled me and warmed my heart.

"I am so sorry, Steven. It was a stupid thing that I did. You have to know that what I did was selfish. My brain was very sick at the time, and I wasn't thinking straight. I hurt you and Dad by trying to end my life, and I'll never forgive myself. Please know that you must never blame yourself in any way. It was my fault. You are my life, and I am so blessed to have you."

He put one arm around me, patted my back, and leaned over me as he scanned the words on the computer screen. And then it dawned on me.

"Hey, Stevie, would you be willing to write about your feelings about what happened that night?"

The writer in him said, "Okay."

* * *

Below is his account of that night:

When I was twelve, my mom tried to kill herself. As far back as I can remember, my mother has been bipolar. She asked me if I would write about that night. It used to be something that frightened me to even talk about it. I still worry about my mom having another episode, but I am trying not to let it affect my life as much as it used to.

One thing that people find interesting is that from the outside, my life appears normal. I maintain an A average in school, start at shortstop on a summer travel team, and play on a travel basketball team. I guess people are confused because some kids seem more affected when faced with a tragedy. Their grades begin to drop and their behavior gets out of hand. Neither of those things happened to me.

Below is my side of the story of the events that took place the night of March 17, 2005:

I huffed and puffed up and down the court of the Westchester County Center as I glanced up at the scoreboard. We were losing 47 to 33. It was hopeless with three minutes left. We trailed by fourteen. I coughed like a seal, and my coach took me out because there was no reason to leave me in. Sitting back in my padded chair, I took a few deep breaths and glanced at my dad sitting in the stands, talking with another parent.

The buzzer sounded and the game was over. It was a miserable night; I felt like I was dead. It was raining cats and dogs outside. It was a dark, mysterious night, and I don't know what it was but there was something in my stomach that left an unpleasant feeling. Why hadn't my mom come to the game? I turned to my father. "Dad, do you know if Mom is okay? She seemed very upset about something today."

He sighed. "Steven, you have to understand something...your mom has been very depressed since this last episode, which started a few months ago. She is still sick."

When we rolled up the driveway, the motion sensors switched on. My dad turned off the radio, and we stepped out of the car. We entered through the garage, pushed open the door to the basement, and the damp, stale air of the basement filled my nostrils. I pushed on the sides of my empty water bottle, pretending it was the blinker on a car, as I sprinted up the stairs and pushed open the door to the hallway. The first thing I saw was the light on in the kitchen. The water was running in the kitchen sink, but my mom wasn't in the kitchen. I noticed my mom's medication bottles on the countertop next to the kitchen sink. All of them were empty except for one.

I quivered with fear. "Dad, something's wrong."

I checked the playroom—empty. I checked the den—empty. The dining room was empty, too. What was going on? I didn't bother to check the living room because we never use it since we have no furniture in there. I sprinted up the carpeted steps and into my room. My dad followed. My room was also empty. We continued to search. She was nowhere.

Finally, we made our way into the master bedroom. She wasn't there either, but the door to the bathroom was closed...and there was a note on the door. "Dad, what does this mean?" We entered the bathroom. The dim light was on, and there was a blanket in the bathtub, but still no sign of my mom.

As my dad silently read the note taped to the door, I watched the corners of his mouth turn down.

"Dad..." I paused. "Where's Mom?"

"I wish I knew where she was."

We went back downstairs and finally opened the doors to the empty living room, which we had not checked yet. Sure enough, there she was, lying on the cold wooden floor, her arms and legs spread out like the points of a star. She was dressed in all black and had a glass next to her with a few drops of water beside the glass. I screamed and sprinted into the kitchen. My elbow throbbed with pain because I had banged it on the doorway on the way to the kitchen. I picked up the phone and called 911.

"You have reached the emergency service. How may I help you?" the calming voice asked.

"My…my…my…my…" The words just wouldn't come out of my mouth. I was frozen.

"Hello? Hello?" the voice echoed through the phone.

I sprinted back into the living room and gave the phone to my dad, telling him that the 911 operator was on the phone. My dad had sat my mom up; she looked drugged, drunk, and very pale. We needed more help. I sprinted back into the den and picked up the phone on the other line to call our neighbors, the Hamburgs. They have caller ID so they knew it was me.

"Hey, Steve, what's up?" Rebecca said.

I was crying hysterically. "Put your mom on the phone."

She didn't question me.

"Steve, what's the matter?" Laurie asked.

"When we got back from our basketball game…we couldn't find my mom, and now we just found her lying on the floor…I think she's dead." I broke out into tears.

"Please come over; we need help!"

My neighbors came over right away. Laurie took me back to her house and her husband Steve stayed to help my dad. Before we left, I kissed my mom on the forehead. Then I got down on my knees and put my hands together. "P-p-p-please, Mom, pull through." She opened her eyes and mumbled something.

Laurie and I went back to her house and were greeted by their sweet, energetic dachshund named Lucy. I lay on their couch with a glass of ice water and snuggled with Lucy. Tears continued to drip down my cheeks. Jared, my best friend, came over to me and sat with me on the couch. I remember we watched the Illinois vs. Farleigh Dickinson game.

My stomach churned. For all I knew, my mom could be dead. But she was okay. My dad called from the hospital. She survived. Later, I learned that my mom tried to kill herself. When I visited her in the hospital, I saw her like I never saw her before. She was like a stranger to me. Her suicide attempt raised a question in my head: When will I be able to trust my mom again? This question left an unpleasant feeling in my stomach for months...

(After Steven typed the above description of events, he printed out a copy, handed it to me, and said, "I'm not finished yet. I still have more to add.")

Crazy Eggs and Ham

CHAPTER VII

Morning comes and I roll out of bed. Tess is already gone. The bathroom is mine. The splash of water on my face wakes me up just a little. As I stand in front of the distorted mirror, I see a warped reflection of myself. I resemble the ghoulish figure in Edvard Munch's painting, *The Scream.* Along with the bluish pallor of my skin and the shadowy, sunken circles orbiting my eyes, my mouth opens widely to motion a silent scream. All of my energy has been drained and my spirit—vacated.

Hunger pangs kick in from not eating much the day before, so I head out for some breakfast. Halfway down the hall, I realize that I am still in my snowflake pajamas, but I could care less. The usual spread consists of bagels, fruit salad, and hard-boiled eggs. They also put out juice and hot water for tea and coffee. They only serve caffeinated beverages at breakfast. The rest of the day is just decaf.

When I was young, every Sunday morning my dad used to make my sisters and me crazy eggs and Taylor ham, while my mom got to sleep in. Crazy eggs were my father's own creation. They were scrambled eggs with a secret ingredient that always came from his coffee mug. Years later, I learned that the secret ingredient was either white wine or beer depending upon what was in his coffee mug at the time. He fried some Taylor ham on the side. Taylor ham is a poor man's bacon.

My dad was always up early and dressed by the time we woke up. It wasn't until I was older that I realized the reason he was up so early was because he had never gone to bed the night before. Being of Irish decent, he always loved a good party and took to the drink quite easily. Growing up, his drinking never seemed to faze me—maybe because he was generally a happy drunk. It could also be that he wasn't home enough for it to make an impact.

From what I can remember of him, though, he was a very affectionate dad and welcomed the same. We would sit upon his lap and squeeze his nose while he made funny sounds. He never tired of us sitting on his lap or hanging on his back, and we never tired of his kisses. All he asked in return was a good back scratch while he sat on the couch watching the Giants, drinking a beer, and cracking walnuts. He had this huge cyst right smack in the middle of his back that we would press as he made the *ding-dong* sound of a doorbell. My mom once made an attempt to lance the thing herself with nothing but a hot compress and one of her sewing needles. It came back, of course. (Did they ever go the doctor for those things back then?)

During halftime, my younger sister Linda and I would perform for him. While a tune from *The Partridge Family* played in the background, Linda and I would put on a song and dance routine that we'd rehearsed only moments earlier in our bedroom. He always applauded our efforts.

My older sister paints a slightly different picture of my father. Kathleen and I are Irish twins. Even though we were only thirteen months apart, she was born an old soul. From as far back as I can remember, Kathleen was an extremely astute individual. I must admit, my dad did treat her differently because of it. Kath knew of his shenanigans and didn't hesitate to point them out to him or to my mother. "You're just like your mother," he would say to her, or he would call her Mouth if she happened to speak up or offer her opinion.

For example, my mom would ask my father to bring us to the park on Saturdays, which he did—for approximately twenty minutes. Then it was off to the OTB to place some bets. He used to let us pick the horses. Once I picked a racehorse named Snowflake, which happened to win him some money. That's how we got our nicknames, from racehorses. Kathleen was Stardust, I was Snowflake, and Linda was Sunshine. The outing always came to a close with a visit to Uncle Ken's bar, the Gaslight Inn. My dad would sit on a barstool and socialize with friends while we sat at a table sipping our Shirley Temples. Linda and I were none the wiser. We were quite content with our childhood full of Shirley Temples and off-track betting, but Kath knew that something was amiss.

My father was one of those self-made success stories; with very little education and a lot of ambition, he worked his way up the ladder. He was a salesman through and through; he even used to call himself a prostitute because he had to sell himself in order to gain a client. He started out working for a company that sold office furniture in Manhattan. He was a likeable, eager employee, so his boss took him under his wing, and Dad learned the business quickly. Soon he created his own company, RPC, which stood for his initials. I later learned from some of his former colleagues that he was one of the pioneers of the contract interior design industry. He would work from start to finish when a company would move into a new office space, laying out the floor plans, furnishing the space, and then helping the company make the transition into the new offices. He also realized the importance of utilizing space more efficiently by laying out floor plans with cubicles to section office space. At the time, cubicles were a new concept. Dad's projects included many office spaces in Manhattan, Yonkers, and White Plains.

His success afforded him a nibble of the lifestyle he so savored, and it wasn't long before my parents were planning to move out of our cramped apartment in Queens. I remember tagging along while they shopped for a house on the Hudson River with a prominent view of the Tappan Zee Bridge. My father loved to sail and fish. Unfortunately, before we moved, his company went bankrupt due to his drinking and gambling.

I was eleven when my parents told us they were going to separate. Children know nothing of this term. They nonchalantly explained that Daddy would not be living with us anymore. We would see him on weekends instead. In unison, the three of us let out an inconsolable cry.

He tried to comfort us. "This has nothing to do with you girls. Your mom and I love you very much, and that will never change."

Mom continued the explanation. "It's just that your dad and I don't love each other like husband and wife anymore, and we think it's best if Daddy moves out."

It was at that very moment that the world drastically changed for three little girls. No more summers in the Bahamas. No more hotel suites rented to watch the St. Patrick's Day parade. No more dinners at Tavern on the Green. No more horse and buggy rides in Central Park. Most of all, there would be no more crazy eggs and ham.

My older self now understands what a difficult decision it must have been for my mother to separate from my father. With very few skills, she returned to the workforce full-time to raise three children on her own. The only thing she felt proficient in at the time was sewing, so she found employment in the fabric department of our local department store, Robert Hall. Pulling twelve-hour shifts six days a week, my mother was eventually promoted to manager of the fabric department. For sanity's sake, putting in the long days of work was worth it to her. In truth, my father was an alcoholic and a big-time gambler, and my mom felt it was toxic for all of us to be around him. He basically drank and gambled his entire life away—including his three little girls.

Of course, in the beginning, my father made the occasional attempts to see us, but it wasn't long before his presence faded altogether. There was always speculation as to his whereabouts. Did he have another life somewhere? Did he possibly have another family? Maybe we had half-brothers and sisters out there. I even convinced myself that he was a spy who had been exposed and had to flee to protect us from any harm. I suppose the latter was the result of watching too many *Get Smart* episodes and James Bond movies.

Years later, once we were all grown up, my father came back to us. He was at a place in his life where he felt the need to make amends. The twelve-step program had finally reached him. Linda and I were open to his request for a visit, although Kath was not so accommodating. My curiosity was piqued. I wanted to meet the man who was once my fun-loving dad. I had already forgiven him for leaving us. I came to understand that his alcoholism was an illness, which in turn created the downward spiral in his life.

Over the years of dealing with my bipolar condition, I have met many alcoholics and drug addicts in the ACU. Interestingly, I learned that sometimes those who struggle with a mental illness may also self-medicate with alcohol and/or drugs and then end up with an addiction to boot. Reflecting back on his cycles, I suspect my father also struggled with a bipolar condition. Back then, however, no one ever spoke of such things. The term *bipolar* was not mainstream, but *crazy* and *cuckoo* were. Those labels never come easily for anyone.

After the birth of my son, my father would visit from time to time. During one visit, we ended up having a heart-to-heart over our past. I learned that he'd lived the life of a transient, roaming from state to state. At times, he sought refuge with the Salvation Army.

"Things were really bad back then," he said to me. "You see, I owed the wrong people a lot of money, and, if you know what I mean, they were not so understandin' when I couldn't pay them back. Late one night when I was leavin' my office, a bullet shot right through my briefcase, and I fell to my knees.

Two men came up behind me and made it very clear that they wanted their money. I was beaten with a golf club—left me black n' blue all over. My kneecaps were destroyed, and they left me half-dead on the curb—cause if they killed me, they knew they'd never get their money back."

As he described this incident, I recalled exactly when it happened. It was right before he moved out; he walked with crutches for a few weeks. He had made light of it and told us he had been in a barroom brawl.

Tears began to well up in his eyes as he continued. "I left you girls to protect you from myself and from others. I was a failure and a worthless drunk. I was not worthy of being your father."

His story appeared to be a convenient explanation, but then he looked at me with an expression of complete remorse. "I never meant to hurt you girls. I thought you would be better off without me. I'm sorry." He choked up. "I am so sorry."

"I've already forgiven you," I replied, as if my pardon were some sort of grand gesture given by a high priestess.

Our cordial relationship lasted about a year. After my first nervous breakdown, my father became an apparition in my life once again. My insanity must have struck a familiar chord in him. He even told me he blamed himself for passing on his bad genes. In some respects, the second abandonment came as an even heavier blow to me than the first. Twelve years have passed since then. Twelve years of going in and out of manic-depressive episodes, twelve years of being routinely hospitalized, and still no sign of my father. But as I sit here in the psych ward reflecting on my suicide attempt, I see my father standing before me clear as day.

I rise to my feet to gaze into the eyes of this man standing before me, not quite knowing whether his presence is real or imaginary. At this point, it doesn't really matter, because I now face him, not from the standpoint of his abandoned child nor as his judge, but I stand *with* him on equal ground—the ground that is the plantation of human imperfection. I stand with him as a parent with a hefty transgression against my own child that warrants resolution.

With tears in my eyes and a lump in my throat, I reach out and hold my father's hand.

Now I completely understand him...I completely understand.

Transients

CHAPTER VIII

As you can see, drifting from past to present to future and back again is easy to do when you're in a psychiatric ward. At times, these three states collapse into one and the same.

At present, I finish eating breakfast and curl up in my familiar chair. I savor the last cup of caffeinated coffee and turn on the TV to watch the news. Sitting here, in this very same chair, reminds me of yet another previous hospital visit. I was watching the news and noticed a new patient sitting across from me. It was obvious he was in bad shape. There was something familiar about him, but I couldn't quite put my finger on it. He looked like a homeless person. He was dressed in hospital-like scrubs and those light blue socks with the grip strips on the bottom that they give to patients who typically arrive unexpectedly or by court order. The greasy strands of his hair were going every which way, and his lanky form slouched to one side of the chair.

He stared blankly at the television, and I followed suit. The usual headlines were on the news—roadside bombings, local burglaries, bears being rescued out of trees, etc. Then I saw him. There he was—simultaneously on television and sitting right next to me in the Day Room—a longtime actor who'd been arrested for crashing his car while reportedly being heavily intoxicated. The mugshot on television bore a striking resemblance to the image of the man sitting across from me. He got up to switch channels, but to no relief. His mugshot was being plastered all over the airwaves. He looked over at me, shook his head, and mumbled in his distinct deep, raspy voice, "I never take a good picture." I smiled timidly as he turned to seek refuge in his room.

Before I was diagnosed as crazy, I lived a quiet existence at home in Queens with my mother and two sisters. During my early twenties, I worked as a litigation secretary for a law firm in Manhattan while I went to college part-time. When you live in one of the outer boroughs and work in Manhattan, mass transit is the obvious choice for commuters. You would think, though, that Queens would be a quick hop, skip, and a jump to Manhattan, but it took me at least an hour to get to work. First, I would take a bus to Long Island City, then transfer to the 7 train, and then switch to the 4, 5, or 6—all this just to get to the midtown area. Commuting provided a wealth of opportunity to study the faces of my fellow commuters. Some people drank their coffee. Some enjoyed a muffin or a bagel on their way in. Some women applied their makeup or painted their nails en route. Some people read their newspapers, avoiding all possible eye contact. Keep in mind, back in the early eighties, there were no cell phones, no iPods, no gadgets resembling a

BlackBerry. This left commuters no choice but to look through one another to gaze out the windows. Even to this day, there is a quiet understanding amongst commuters that conversation is not part of the everyday commuting etiquette, unless you're stuck in a dark tunnel somewhere. Then you need to make friends really fast.

I have to admit, I was never a morning person. The snooze button on my alarm clock was my favorite feature, so the race was on every morning to make the bus. As a seasoned commuter, I employed all of the timesaving, multitasking techniques mentioned above. Once I was in such a hurry to get to work, I dressed quickly, opened the door to my closet, and without looking down, slipped on my shoes. My sprint to the bus stop was clocked as one of my personal best. I used to make a mental note of my timing and technique. Why did I challenge myself in this way? I made my way onto the bus and sat down, proud of my accomplishment. Then I switched from bus to subway. The commuters were jammed into car of the train, but luckily a woman rose up to exit the train. Since I was strap-hanging over her, I was advantageously positioned to inherit her seat— another basic commuter rule. I was thinking this could be one of those days where red lights turn green in a domino-like sequence, but while I was reveling in my commuter conquests, I noticed people looking down at my feet. There I was with one black shoe on my left foot and one white shoe on my right. The embarrassment lasted only as long as it took for me to get to a shoe store and buy a brand new pair of shoes. Needless to say, I was late to work that morning.

You have to be in Manhattan during rush hour to appreciate the orchestrated chaos of the hustle and flow. With blind eyes, we retrace our steps every day. Sometimes we are too absorbed in our own so-called problems to notice those among us who don't comply with the "normal" standards. During my travels, I came across some of these transient individuals, the ones that we pass by with averted eyes. Sometimes I wonder who the real transients are—them or us. They are the homeless. Some are addicts, some are physically handicapped, and some are mentally ill—just to name a few.

I remember taking comfort in knowing that I was not one of them. I wasn't like the man on the train who wore alien antennae with crumpled up tinfoil balls on top. He would tell the commuters he was from a faraway planet and had come to earth to soothe us with his saxophone. Through his music, he would send us the positive vibrations of the universe. I always felt compelled to give him spare change for his creativity.

I also took comfort in knowing I wasn't like the man who lived in the subway tunnels during the winter months. I wasn't the wino who cleared out an entire subway car because his stench was too much to bear. I wasn't like the old woman who sat outside of her cardboard box on the sidewalk with a sign that read "Will work 4 food."

I passed by these individuals every day on my way to work, wondering how they got to such a place. Some mornings, I would give my coffee and bagel to the old woman holding the sign. She looked like the typical bag lady with her layered, disheveled clothing and a shopping cart filled with all of her worldly possessions—mostly made up of old blankets and recyclables. As I would hand her my breakfast, she would reach up with her arthritic hand and say, "Bless you, my dear." Aside from her dreary appearance, she wore this purple bracelet that sparkled along with her blue eyes. One rainy morning when I gave her my breakfast, she gave me the purple bracelet in return. I told her that I couldn't take it, but she insisted.

"No, no, please take it," she said. "I don't need it anymore. You see, it used to be green. Green is the color of insanity. Now it's purple. Purple is the color of healing. I'm all better now. So, I'm moving on. Keep the bracelet until you feel you don't need it anymore. Then pass it on."

I thanked her for the bracelet, and she thanked me for the food. I put the bracelet in my raincoat pocket and chalked up her words as crazy talk from a homeless person. The very next morning, gone from the subway grate was the cardboard box. Gone was the shopping cart. Gone was the old lady. I never saw her again.

Years later, after I was diagnosed with bipolar disorder, I was cleaning out my coat closet deciding what should go to charity. I came across the old raincoat, and like every other coat, I checked the pockets before putting it in the pile. I found the purple bracelet, and the old lady's words came flooding back to me, only this time with much more meaning.

I realize now that I am that old woman with only a few exceptions. The line that separates us is faint. Without the support of my loved ones, I could be the one sitting on that same sidewalk. Without my medications, I could be the one picking the trashcans for redeemables. Without proper health insurance, I could be among those we turn a blind eye to in the street.

I gave the raincoat away to the Salvation Army, but I kept the purple bracelet.

Group

CHAPTER IX

After my coffee, I return briefly to my room to clean myself up and put on some clothes so as not to look like one of the aforementioned transients. An announcement comes over the loudspeaker.

"The morning group session starts in ten minutes. All patients are expected to attend."

In the ACU, we're all lumped together—the drug addicts, the alcoholics, the cutters, those with eating disorders, those with obsessive compulsive disorders, those with major depression, those who are completely manic, etc. I think you get the picture.

The subject of this morning's session is art therapy. We are given a topic or a feeling and asked to express it through a drawing. Today, we're supposed to draw how we feel in the present moment. I don't mind art therapy. Drawing is something I've excelled in since I was a young girl. It allows for introspection.

What's amusing is that it also allows for interpretation by the therapist and others in the group.

After a few minutes of drawing time, you can choose to present your work to the group. This session, I quickly draw a giant question mark in bubble formation and color it in with green and purple stripes. I spend the rest of the time observing others in the group. My attention turns to the counselor, who, based on her age and enthusiasm, must be a newbie.

"Janine, would you like to show your drawing?" the counselor asks.

I hold up my drawing and say nothing.

"I see you drew a colorful question mark. What does it represent?"

"What do you think it represents?" I question.

"Well, I think it represents a question that you may have."

"Interesting," I say with a sarcastic tone.

"What is your question?" she asks.

I point to the drawing. "That is the question."

"What question?" she asks confused.

"I'm asking you," I reply.

She tilts her head to one side and says, "Wait a minute... wait a minute...I'm asking you. What's your question?"

"I don't know. That's why I'm asking you." I can't resist being difficult.

Frustrated by the banter, she opens the question to the group.

"Would anyone like to comment on Janine's question?"

"What question?" a patient asks.

The counselor clears her throat. "Let me rephrase that. Would anyone like to interpret her drawing of a question mark?" the woman states emphatically.

"It's a question mark with purple and green stripes," said one observant patient.

"I think it represents all of the questions in the universe," Marla comments.

"That's good, Marla," the counselor says. "Would you like to give us an example of a question?"

"Umm, like why the fuck am I here? Like, why the fuck don't people understand that I like to cut myself? It's my body and I should be able to do whatever the fuck I want to my own body. I'm not hurting anyone else. So why the fuck should I have to be put in a place like this?"

The counselor interrupts, "Okay, Marla, thanks for those examples. Would anyone else like to comment?"

"Yeah, she's right! Why do we have to be in this place?" Tim aka the nose picker exclaims. "We're like caged animals. And why do we have to do these stupid drawings? And why can't we have more deck time?"

"Yeah, that's right! Why can't we have more deck time?" says another disgruntled patient.

It is apparent the rookie counselor is overwhelmed by these questions. "I'll make a note of your requests and pass them on to the administration." She scribbles away on her clipboard. "Now let's move on to another drawing."

At this point, the group discussion is a bit out of her control. I feel bad that I might have incited the uprising.

The Raven turns to me and whispers, "Did you draw a question mark just to be difficult?"

"Maybe...I don't know. I was just too lazy to draw anything else."

The group simmers down as we focus on another drawing.

"Margaret," the counselor asks, "what did you draw?"

I am curious to see if Margaret's drawing will give us an insight into her world. I am not disappointed.

She turns over her drawing, holds it up slightly with her weak, scrawny arms, and says, "Just like me, this is what gravity will do to all of you one day."

Margaret has drawn a quick sketch of an old woman sitting on a stool, nude, with both breasts sagging and splayed out to their respective sides. In the sketch, the woman's legs fall open like a book, revealing a multitude of layers and folds that comprise her vagina.

There's a slight chuckle amongst the group.

"Go ahead. Laugh now...but this is your inevitable demise," Margaret says in a melancholy voice. "Enjoy your bodies now. One day you'll look like this, and then you'll see. Your significant other will tire of it. Soon they'll find another spring chicken to replace you."

The group quiets. We all know there is truth in her statement.

"That's very telling, Margaret," the counselor comments. "Good job. Thanks for sharing with us." Turning to Tess, the counselor asks, "Would you like to show us your drawing?"

From across the room, Tess raises up the drawing she has been working on since I met her. It's a self-portrait made up entirely of tiny multicolored dots. It looks exactly like her.

For some strange reason, Tess fixes her gaze upon me. "I'm not finished yet," she mumbles. "It needs more dots."

Everyone looks at the drawing in awe.

"The detail is amazing! It certainly looks finished to me," says the counselor, obviously impressed.

Tess glances at the counselor for a second and replies, "No... no...it's not. It's flawed. Can't you see that? It needs more work." Then Tess refocuses her attention back to me and says, "Right, Janine? Just like you—it's flawed."

"What?" I say, confused. "Who the hell are you to tell me I'm flawed? You don't know me."

"Oh, but I do," she says hauntingly. "I know more about you than you think."

"Really...like what?"

"Like, you snore."

The group laughs.

"I also know that you bite your nails like a nervous child."

I nod.

"I also know that you have some sort of sick affinity for those snowflake pajamas of yours. Like, what's up with that? Did you lose your virginity in them or something? They look like they haven't been washed in decades. They're so fucking gross."

"Okay," the counselor interjects. "Let's not focus on the negative."

Tess ignores her and continues. "Oh yeah...I also know that you absolutely loathe yourself for trying to off yourself."

"What!" I yell. "Who the hell are you? You don't know me!"

"Oh, please, give me a break. I know you, Janine," she remarks in a calm *little-miss-know-it-all* way. "I know your type.

Oh poor you, with your perfect little family and your whiny little ways. Do you think they deserve what you did to them?"

The counselor interrupts again. "Okay, time to move on. Let's not dwell on the negative."

But by this point, I am filled with rage. Even though I know Tess is right, who is she to judge me? I mean, seriously, who the hell is she?

I shout at her, "You have no clue! *No fucking clue!* You think you know me? You don't know me."

"Okay, whatever you say, Janine," Tess replies apathetically.

This only enrages me further. I become even louder. "You don't know me! How could you? You haven't pulled your head out of your ass or out of your fucking dots long enough to pass judgment on me!"

Tess just sits there with complete composure. *I hate her.*

As I continue my rant, I notice from the corner of my eye the counselor motioning for one of the health techs, Phil, to come over. I know what that means.

Phil leans over me and taps my shoulder. "Come on, Janine. Let's take a little walk."

"Oh yeah...right...this is great. Why am I the one who gets to go to the Quiet Room?" I protest. "She's the bitch who started all of this!" I point at Tess. "You're such a bitch—*such a bitch!*"

As Phil escorts me out of the Day Room, the counselor circumvents the group's attention. "Let's get back to the drawings, shall we? I think your self-portrait is amazing! Did you decide to draw your portrait in a multitude of dots because you are a very complex, multifaceted individual?"

"Uh...no," I hear Tess say, and I look back to see her wearing a smug little smirk while her eyes follow me out the door. "I just like making dots."

The session ends, and everyone scatters like the tiny little dots on a page made up of a broad spectrum of color filled with many question marks.

The Quiet Room

CHAPTER X

With one hand, Phil continues to lead me out of the Day Room while he fishes for the key to the Quiet Room with the other.

"Did you see her? Did you see how she provoked me?" I shriek.

"Yeah, yeah...I know, Janine." Phil's not stupid. He's done this one too many times to know never to argue with an irate crazy person.

"She's evil. She has no soul," I say to him as he ushers me into the Quiet Room.

"In you go, Janine. Why don't you just take a little time out for yourself and try to calm down."

"A time-out? I don't need a time-out. What am I, three years old?" I shout.

"Now, Janine, you know the quicker you calm down, the quicker you can come out."

"Phil, you better make sure that Dr. Kissilenko knows I'm in here," I demand. "And make sure that I get a different room away from *her* when I get out!"

"Will do," he whispers with his pointer pressed to his lips as he quietly backs out of the Quiet Room and locks the door.

I feel like a caged animal as I pace back and forth. Peering out the small cut-out window, I pound on the locked door, demanding to be heard, but to no avail. Defeated and deflated, I collapse onto the old, torn gym mat. I am no stranger to this room. In fact, Phil had been my escort here during a previous hospital visit. This barren room is quite deceiving. To the naked eye, it's an eight by twelve empty room, but I know otherwise. It's not empty. I may have been left alone here to my own devices, but my own devices will not leave me alone. An invitation to the Quiet Room is the perfect opportunity for all of my fun loving companions to pay me a visit.

So let's get this tea party started. Out rolls the table. I set down and smooth out the table linens and put out the fine china and heirloom teapot that, against my will, has been handed down from generation to generation. My guests arrive forthwith.

Allow me to introduce to you my favorite cast of characters. To my right is my guest of honor. He's a handsome young man with carefree, light brown hair. He is over six feet tall and wears wrinkled, distressed clothing, yet he is fresh and clean looking. From time to time, he visits me in my sleep. As I go in and out of twilight sleep, I see glimpses of him as he looms quietly over me. I never feel afraid when he's around, yet he's hard to read. I can't figure out what he wants from me. Sometimes he smiles sweetly at me, while other times he looks at me with curiosity, trying to read me as well. We never have any verbal exchange. Our relationship is on a much higher level. I feel safe with him. I have not, and never will, give him a name, for I suspect he is not from this earth.

To my left is another apparition. She is not so friendly. She also visits me in my sleep but is not so thoughtful. She jolts me out of sleep with her face only inches from mine, wearing an angry face with bulging eyes and a clenched jaw. Her hair frays out in all directions, making for a frightful appearance. Like my male friend to the right, she has no name and does not speak. She does, however, growl at me. At first when she growled, I would jump up out of bed and shriek; then she would return that very same night to harass me. But with each visit, I became wise to her ways and decided to fight back. One night as I opened my eyes, there she was, as usual, inches from my face, growling. I lifted my head off the pillow, looked straight into her eyes, and echoed her growl. Her image froze and then melted away. Even though she still visits me on occasion, I just growl back at her now and she leaves me in peace for the rest of the night.

My third guest sits across from me. It's a fetus that looks to be about eight weeks old. Unlike my other guests, the fetus talks to me, but we always seem to have the same conversation over and over again.

"What's my name?" the fetus asks.

"I don't know," I reply.

"Yes...you do."

"No, I don't."

"My name is Daniel. Say it. Say my name."

"Okay, your name is Daniel."

"Say it again."

"Daniel," I repeat.

"Again," he insists.

"*Daniel!*" I shout.

"That's right. That's my name. Don't ever forget it."

"I won't, Daniel. I promise. I'll never forget your name."

But strangely enough, like many recurring dreams, every time he comes to visit me, I can never remember his name. We systematically engage in this same conversation.

The tea party eventually comes to an end as I bid farewell to my guests, knowing that I will see them all in good time. There's nothing left to do but to lie listless on the old gym mat.

Surrender

CHAPTER XI

After spending part of the morning in the Quiet Room, the rest of the day drones on in the usual way with one lovely exception—a healthy dose of an anti-anxiety medication which they encourage me to take before exiting the Quiet Room. It doesn't take long for the drug to kick in, and I am *feeling good* and free to roam about the unit.

During deck time, I recline on the bench right next to Petey, who is playing guitar. Even though it's the middle of March in the middle of the day, I deem it fitting to sing "Oh Holy Night." As I lie there on my back, gazing up at the heavens with hands raised, I belt out, *"Oh holy night, the stars are brightly shining. It is the night of our dear Savior's birth..."*

Petey interjects with all the precise guitar chords just like I knew he would. We are the perfect pair. We should go on the road. Our audience gathers around, forming a semicircular ring with the haze of cigarette smoke shielding their identities. I rise up from the bench to gain the strength for such a challenging vocal and continue, *"Long lay the world in sin and error pining, till He appeared and the soul felt its worth. A thrill of hope, the weary world rejoices, for yonder breaks a new and glorious morn."* Then for full effect, I fall to my knees. *"Fall on your knees. Oh hear the angels' voices. Oh night divine, oh night when Christ was born, oh night divine...oh night...oh night divine..."*

With my finish comes applause and adulation from the crowd. One fan walks over to me and says, "Janine, I need to shake your hand. You really made my day."

I don't know her name and am surprised she knew mine. Since I've been here, I've noticed that she has never opened her mouth to anyone—except to herself. Every time I see her, I notice that she has a running, angry dialogue with herself—yet she knows my name. Wow, I must be good. But don't take my word for it. Petey even told me so. It was my finest hour.

After receiving such praise out on the deck, it's time to return to the Day Room. During lunch, I bask in my newfound celebrity status, complete with an entourage. We are discussing which song I should sing during the next deck break, when I am interrupted by my doctor.

"Ms. Haynes, may I have a moment with you?"

I turned to my posse and say with a wink, "I'll be right back. Make sure no one touches my food. That includes you, Tim!"

My doctor and I walk out of the Day Room and into the Music Room for a private consultation.

"So, Ms. Haynes, I heard you had a trying morning. You had a few outbursts in the group session and spent some time in the Quiet Room."

"Yeah, but it's all good now. What was that they gave me, Ativan?"

"Yes. Well, I'm happy to hear it helped to calm you down. What I want now is to talk to you about your recent suicide attempt. I highly recommend that you undergo electroconvulsive therapy. I know that I have recommended it to you in the past when you've been severely depressed, but I think it's something you should seriously consider."

In the past, I have always shot down the idea of shock treatment. Remnants of the movie *One Flew Over the Cuckoo's Nest* haunt me to this day. I remember watching the scene in which Jack Nicholson's character is forced to have shock treatment. They drag him into the room, strap him down, stick things on his head, and shove a bit in his mouth while sending electrical shockwaves to his temples. His entire body convulses while he remains conscious the entire time. The cruelty of it all made a major impact on me and has lasted to this day.

My doctor reassures me that the process is not as cruel as they depict in the movie. He reminds me that the movie was made in 1975, and the technology and the way in which they administer shock treatment has come a long way since then. They don't call it shock treatment anymore. It has a kinder, gentler name—electroconvulsive therapy (ECT).

Anri Kissilenko has been treating me for several years now. His official title is Chief of Adult and Geriatric Services at Silver Hill Hospital. He is a gentle, gentle man who speaks with a Bulgarian accent that is soothing to the ear; his accent even makes shock treatment sound inviting. He never makes me feel like a crazy person. There is a sense of trust. Having faith in a doctor is incredibly important to the recovery process, especially if you have paranoiac tendencies.

He explains, in his accent, the ECT process in a methodical way. "First, you will walk to the treatment room in the morning and lie down on the bed. The nurse will attach a blood pressure cuff and EEG and EKG leads in order to monitor your pressure and heart rate. I will then swab your forehead and temples and attach the electrodes. I will then ask you to breathe in oxygen through a mask while the anesthesiologist administers the general anesthesia intravenously, and you will be unconscious throughout the entire treatment."

"How long will I be under anesthesia?" "About twenty minutes, and then you will wake up right in here in this very room, the Music Room. Do you have any questions, Ms. Haynes?"

"Do you strap me down while I get shocked?"

"No, no. After you are unconscious, we will administer a muscle relaxant which prevents the spasms. We will, however, put in a mouth guard so when you seizure, you will not bite your tongue."

"What do you mean by seizure?"

"Once the electric current is administered, it forces the seizure, which helps to correct the imbalance in your brain. The seizure lasts for about thirty seconds."

"Will I lose my memory?"

"Depending upon how many treatments you have, there will be some short-term memory that will be lost during the series of treatments. For example, you may forget conversations you might have, a person's name, or appointments. Sometimes, there is also some long-term memory loss as well."

"How many treatments will I need?"

"At first, the treatments will be intensive. Three times a week for the first couple of weeks; depending upon your progress, we will reduce the treatments to once a week, then once every two weeks, then once per month and so on."

I breathe in deep and contemplate. Why am I so afraid of shock treatment? After a suicide attempt, low voltages of electrical currents running through my body don't sound so frightening. I also take into consideration the attendance of my three guests at the tea party in the Quiet Room. Without further delay, I make my decision.

"Sure, why not? Let's give it a go."

"Very good," he replies. "I can arrange for you to speak with other patients receiving ECT. That may help to reassure you."

"Am I going to have to stay in the hospital long?"

"Depending on how you progress, you can be discharged and continue to receive ECT on an outpatient basis."

Later on, I end up talking with a few patients who are receiving ECT, and they all appear to have their sanity intact. One patient I meet comes in every month for what they call maintenance treatment. We talk briefly, and she tells me how she did not want to take a chance of slipping into a major depression ever again.

I watch as she goes into the treatment room and wait approximately twenty minutes for her to come out. They wheel her out, unconscious, on a gurney and roll her into the Music Room, which also serves as the Recovery Room. They pull down the shades on the glass windows to the room, and a tech sits by the door, waiting for her to wake up. When she wakes up, they give her some water and help her walk around. They check her blood pressure and bring her a bagel and juice. She nibbles away while sitting on a chair that leans against the wall of the Fishbowl. I sit down beside her.

"How are you feeling?" I ask her.

"I'm fine…just a little groggy."

"Are you going to be able to drive home?"

She looks at me with confusion. "I'm sorry, do I know you? Are you a doctor?"

I'm not sure what to say, so I just smile and say, "No."

As I walk away, I entertain the thought of having certain parts of my memory obliterated. It's certainly tempting to erase the memories leading up to this moment. I wouldn't mind forgetting who and what I have become. It would certainly come as a relief to me if the shock treatment could erase the guilt, the pain, and the heartache of my actions.

Why should I fight against it? What do I have to lose? Is it worth losing some memories? Would it be so terrible to sacrifice some of the good memories along with some of the bad in exchange for some peace of mind?

I've run out of options. I am beyond desperate. I have no strength to fight anymore.

I schedule my first shock treatment for tomorrow morning.

I surrender…*I completely surrender.*

Anecdotes of a Crazy Person, with Love from Your Husband

CHAPTER XII

Once again, I just want to jump ahead briefly to a year and a half after my suicide attempt, when I decided to write this memoir. After months of writing about my life as a crazy person, my husband finally decided to read it. This chapter is brought to you by my husband, Larry. He thought it was fitting to insert it here to enlighten you, the reader, just in case you haven't already gotten the picture as to how crazy I can actually be.

For months, Larry put off reading my story. He would say to me, "I don't have to read it, Janine. I've lived it. Remember?" He was certainly right. I understood where he was coming from, but it bothered me that he didn't care enough to read it. By this point, I had circulated my work to some close friends and family. Everyone was so receptive and encouraged me to continue writing. I assumed my husband would follow suit. To this day, we've never really discussed, at length, how he felt about my suicide attempt. I thought that if he read my story, it would give us the opportunity to talk about it.

Once he finally read it, he had no comment or feedback—negative or otherwise. Aside from my son's opinion, my husband's opinion was the one that I needed badly, like a druggie needs a fix, and he wasn't giving it to me. So one night, I got up the nerve to broach the subject. My heart began to race, and if you listened closely, you could detect the cracking in my voice. I was afraid, not because he's a monster, but because I knew that he would be the one to tell me honestly what he thought. That's one thing about Lar—he's honest. Sometimes honesty can hurt. His other shining attributes are his strength and character. I must admit that he is the superglue that has kept our family together for almost twenty years, whereas I am the crazy glue. Please don't be mistaken—our marriage has endured more than its fair share of issues that many couples experience when together for a long period of time; but our marriage has an added bonus feature—my bipolar condition. My husband can truly say, without hesitation, that he is married to a loon and actually mean it. Needless to say, being crazy helps spice up the relationship. We are never bored. It may sound sappy, but I am in love with him more now than I was when we were first married. When we exchanged vows, he took the *in sickness and in health* part seriously. At times, he has played the role of my guardian, my doctor, and, dare I say it, a father figure as well. We sat down one Friday evening to unwind and watch a little TV.

With a bit of the jitters, I began with my opening, "So, did you finish my story?"

"Yeah, I finished it," he said in a short, blunt manner.

"Well, what did you think?" I waited with bated breath.

"It was good, but..."

Oh, holy Moses, Jesus, Mary, and St. Joseph, here it comes.

"I think your story should include more stories of when you are manic and psychotic so the reader can really get into your head and understand just how completely out of your fucking mind you can be."

I paused and tried to remain open. "Okay...give me some examples."

It was like watching the floodgates of heaven open up as Larry began to rattle off the anecdotes of my psychotic episodes.

"Like the time you thought you were our son. At the time, Steven was nine or ten, and you dressed up in his sweatshirt and put on his baseball cap and walked around the house impersonating him."

I burst out laughing. "Get out!" I shrieked. "Are you serious? What did I do?"

"You spoke in a childlike voice and demanded, '*I want pancakes!*' just like Steven used to do."

I continued my laughter. "Oh my God! I really did that?"

"That's not all. At that point, I knew it was time to bring you to the hospital, but you kept stamping your feet like you were a little kid, saying, 'No! I not going!' After a couple of hours of trying to persuade you, I simply said, 'Janine, if you don't get in the car right now, I'm going to call the police.'" He paused for a moment and then remarked, "It's funny. It just goes to show you that as *far out* as you were, your sanity kicked in. The fear of the police coming to get you made you jump right in the car, and we left for the hospital. On the way to the hospital, you rolled down the window and screamed in your baby voice, 'Help! I'm being kidnapped!' Once we finally got to the hospital, you turned to me and said in your meek, childlike voice, 'Ya tricked me. I thought you were bringing me to school.'"

We were both in stitches with tears of laughter streaming down our faces as he gave another account of my craziness.

"There was another time when you were manic, and you went out and bought a bunch of outdoor welcome mats and laid them down in front of each door to every room in the house, for whatever reason—I have no idea."

"Huh, I don't remember that. What else?" I salivated as I searched for a pen and paper. "This is good material. I've got to write this stuff down for my story or I'll forget."

"There was another time when you were in the hospital and you laid in front of the entrance door to the ACU for hours because you said you were receiving messages from under the crack of the door. The staff tried to get you up from the floor, but after awhile, they gave up and just let you stay there."

He then recharged to take in some oxygen and exhaled more stories. "Remember the time of your first breakdown? You were up for days, cleaning at all hours of the night. You weren't eating. You began to hallucinate. You believed aliens were trying to use human bodies as hosts, like in that movie *Invasion of the Body Snatchers*. You thought they were trying to inhabit Steven's body. You also thought your mother and your sister Linda were demons and the Colombian drug lords were after us."

My smile slowly diminished as I sat taking notes in the stenography I learned in high school.

"Then there was the time that you came home from the hospital not quite well yet, and the doctors had you heavily medicated on a drug that gave you side effects that made you tremble like you had Parkinson's."

"I remember that," I replied. "It's gotta be incredibly difficult for people who live day in and day out with the tremors and spasms of Parkinson's disease. Living with those tremors for only a few weeks helped me to understand what it's like to be completely out of control of your physical body. I never felt as uncomfortable in my own skin as I did when I was on that medication."

"Another time you woke me up and said, 'There's somebody in the house!' You jumped up out of bed, looked out our bedroom door, and then jumped back into bed and pulled the covers up with only your eyes exposed and turned to me and said, 'Don't worry. I've got it covered.'"

"And, then there was the time that you opened the window to the second floor bedroom and just sat out on the ledge of the window, swaying side to side."

Like it was a banquet, Larry continued to serve up more anecdotes. Soon, my belly was too full to feast on even the slightest morsel. If I took one more bite, I would retch. I wanted him to stop, but then again, I'd asked for it.

"Then there was another time when we were watching a movie, and you turned to me out of the blue and asked me, 'In the movie *The Stepford Wives*, don't the wives kill their husbands?'"

My original tears of laughter turned into tears of sorrow. "I really said that? How scary is that?"

"Tell me about it. After you went to sleep that night, I went straight downstairs and hid every knife in the house and slept with one eye open. Another night, Steven and I slept in the master bedroom with the door barricaded while you paced back and forth in the hallway for hours. I remember Steven was the one to ask me to block the door. He felt so bad about it and said to me, 'This isn't right, Daddy. This just isn't right. I feel bad.' The next day we took you to the hospital."

As these stories poured out, I finally became aware of what it must be like for him. Not only has Larry been my protector, he has also been the protector for our son and himself. He admitted to me that there were times when he knew he should have brought me to the hospital sooner, but he struggled with the decision to institutionalize his wife over and over again, year after year. Not many people would or could endure a life with a crazy person, yet all these years, he's made it look so easy. He always had 'round the clock help for Steven. He kept Steven's life and schedule as normal as possible, and without skipping a beat, he helped our son with his homework, helped coach his baseball teams, and made sure our family circle remained whole.

As I wrote this song of mine, which now sounds a bit screechy to me, I selfishly wanted him to get into my mind and understand my plight. What I didn't realize was that his melody had been softly playing as background music all these years. How small I feel in comparison to my husband. How large a heart can one person have? How unwavering a creature is he?

And, how privileged I am to be able to call him my husband.

See No Evil, Hear No Evil, Speak No Evil—Feel No Evil

CHAPTER XIII

After making the decision to undergo ECT, I trek several times around the Circle. My thoughts bring me back to an incident that happened a few months earlier. One day, while I was chatting with a friend on the phone, I reclined on a lounge chair in my backyard, basking in the unusual warmth of an early December morning. It was then that I heard a very loud but indistinct birdcall. I rose from the lounge chair and followed the birdcall down the steps that lead to the driveway. There it was—the biggest, most beautiful bird I had ever seen. It was the size of a peacock but without the long tail feathers. Maybe it was a peahen, but I don't think they run wild in suburbia New York. Its overall color was gray with iridescent greens, blues, and purples.

While I was watching this bird, I described it to my friend, Cindy, who was still on the phone. As I moved closer, it began to waddle down my driveway. So I followed it. I looked around to see if anyone else witnessed this beautiful vision, but no one was in sight. I ran back inside to search for my camera, but to no avail. When I returned, the bird was sauntering down the road and then disappeared into the woods down by the stream. I felt privileged to witness such beauty. Enthusiastically, I shared this glorious vision with family and friends. Much to my dismay, they did not seem share the same sense of awe. Rather, an expression of concern was evident on their faces. Two weeks later, I was admitted to the hospital.

To this day, I still believe this bird I encountered was real. Sometimes I find myself browsing the Internet under the category of *large wild birds* to see if I can make a positive identification. No success to date.

That was the prelude leading up to my previous hospital visit. It was a couple of weeks before Christmas. I was flying so high in a manic state that I tipped into the psychotic realm. Not all bipolars get psychotic. I do—I'm just lucky like that. Psychosis brings along with it certain features—seeing things, hearing things, and feeling things that are not really there. What's tricky about being in this state of mind is deciphering what is real and what is not. It's like having one of those vivid dreams where you wake up feeling like it actually happened.

Psychosis can also put someone into a state of severe paranoia. During one of my episodes, I believed that aliens needed to inhabit our bodies in order for them to survive in the earth's atmosphere. No one believed me. I grappled with my own thinking, trying to rationalize and make sense of it all. I thought to myself, *Aliens? That's absurd! It must be the CIA—it's always the CIA.* I'm certain if psychiatrists took a poll of psychotic patients, it would reveal that the number one paranoia, in one way or another, always involves the CIA. I believed the CIA was keeping track of me through my television, microwave, toaster, and computer. It went without saying that my house and phone were already bugged. I stood as a third party looking on as the logical side of my brain wrestled with my crazy side. Finally, I deduced that it was not the CIA. Why would they care about little old me? I decided that it was most definitely the Colombian drug lords who were after me because I knew they knew that I knew that they used my backyard as a burial ground for the remains of people they killed. And this, my friends, is how the paranoid brain unravels.

The psychotic mind is an interesting thing. The term *losing your mind* is quite fitting. You actually lose control of your thought process. Once that happens, it is hard to trust your own thinking. I knew my thoughts were not right. My thoughts were scrambled, and I made no sense when I spoke. When you're psychotic, it is a constant battle between the rational and the irrational, an endless deciphering of the real and the unreal, a never-ending struggle to determine which voices are the voices that are only in your head.

Sometimes psychosis gives way to beautiful thoughts and visions. Other times, it produces horrific, nightmarish images and feelings. Looking back on my first psychotic episode, I experienced all of the above. I was seeing things, hearing things, and feeling things that weren't really there. Seeing angel wings attached to my son's back was a more pleasing vision than when I saw my husband wearing his brain on the outside his cranium. Hearing a lyrical symphony triumphs over the cacophony of voices in your head that tell you, you do not deserve to live. "It could make your skin crawl" is a common phrase that people use to describe something repulsive. I wonder if that saying has a psychotic origin. I prefer the feeling of fresh, clean water running over my body to the feeling of spiders crawling all over me, but, unfortunately, I don't get to choose.

Some flack may come from saying what I am about to say, but I can't help comparing the psychotic experience to divine revelation. Who decides which visions and/or writings are of divine inspiration and which originate from the deranged mind? When Jesus proclaimed to be the son of God, was he just suffering from delusions of grandeur? Faith has to do with believing in the unknown, the unseen, the unheard, and the intangible. If you have faith in a higher power, could it be construed as *crazy*?

Why should I be the one who gets committed when I declare to be Jesus Christ reincarnated in female form? I truly sympathize with the persecution that Jesus endured. Lord knows, I had a difficult time persuading other psych patients to believe that I was the second coming of Christ. Just because I was a woman in a psychiatric hospital was no reason not to believe in that possibility. Where's the faith? I ask you. Where is the faith?

Most religions are based upon miraculous events. Judaism is rooted in the belief that God worked through Moses to set forth deadly plagues upon Egypt. Subsequently, Moses led God's Chosen out of Egypt into the Promised Land by parting the Red Sea. Christianity believes in variations of the second coming of Christ on Judgment Day, banishing all evil and granting everlasting life. If we were actual witnesses to such miracles in this century, would we choose to believe them? Would we choose to see them? Would we choose to speak of them? Would we choose to feel them deep down in our souls? Or would we be committed to a psychiatric facility for those beliefs?

Call me crazy, but I happen to believe in things unseen, unheard, unspoken, and intangible. I have no other choice.

Electric Storms, Electric Shock, Electric Dreams

CHAPTER XIV

etting back to my present predicament, I enjoy my dinner with my new fan club. We exchange information of a gossipy nature. For example, who's who in the unit, who's out to get whom, which doctors suck, how to sneak in a cell phone, etc. The conversations between the mentally ill can be quite confusing and downright incoherent. Yet we all seem to understand each other on some level.

During the course of our dinner conversation, I get to know some of the patients. Andrea looks to be about forty years old and doesn't stop talking for one second, which wouldn't be so terrible if she did it in a less whiny voice. She is extremely volatile. In a matter of minutes, her mood swings back and forth from being drunk with laughter to sobbing uncontrollably. Then there's Kristen, the Asian American girl who shook my hand after my singing debut. Even though she sits with us, she continues the angry dialogue with herself. Every now and then she looks up at me and smiles, only to withdraw and continue with her angry inner dialogue—I think she's schizophrenic. One of my other fans is Coleen. She's quite charming. She thinks she is a bunny rabbit and wears Playboy-like bunny ears and twitches her nose. She nibbles on tiny morsels just like a rabbit. And then there's Tim, the beloved nose picker, waiting for the leftovers from each of our plates. I'm not exactly sure what he's in for.

Tim decides to take a poll as to which look is better for him—a goatee or a small triangular patch of hair under his lower lip. Tim's scruffiness is testimony to his lengthy stay in the ACU. We unanimously vote for him to shave off all of his facial hair. Tim has status. He has earned the right to shave with a disposable razor, and we are four women with a serious case of razor envy. Our hairy armpits and legs are mere testament to that fact. They may have taken away our right to shave, but at least now we get to live vicariously through Tim.

"Shave it all off, Tim," I say. "And, while you're at it, why not shave your chest hair, too?"

"Oh, that would be great!" Coleen concurs.

"Yeah, a bare chest on men is all the rage!" Andrea adds.

Tim grins. "Well, that settles it then. It all comes off tomorrow, girls."

We applaud in unison.

After such amusing dinner conversation, I shift over to my favorite chair by the window and finish my dessert. There's a fierce thunderstorm rolling through. The rain pours out of the sky while thunder crashes down around us like bombs on a battlefield. The lightning electrifies and cracks the sky in half, spider-veining out into tiny capillaries. The fierce energy of the elements gives rise to the awesome power of the universe.

When it stormed like this, my mother used to say that the gods must be angry. The gods certainly have much to be angry about. For millennia, we humans have stormed this planet like we own it. Who are the gods angrier with? The ones who are at war killing each other for one cause or another, or the others who sit back and watch it happen? I want to believe that there is more good than evil in this world, but it's difficult. I lose hope so often when I see the devastation of war, greed, hunger, poverty, and disease. Watching the news enlightens me as to why much of the world hates us these days. Aside from religious differences, there are other divisive issues that play a role. Take the Middle East, for instance. On the news, a reporter was standing in front of what looked to be a pile of rubble—but it was someone's home. In John Lennon's song, "Imagine," there's a line that goes, *"Imagine no possessions. I wonder if you can."* These people don't have to imagine it. It is their reality.

Watching the news only makes me feel even more guilty and depressed for whining and complaining about my life and my illness. Instead of feeling like a burden on society, I would rather be one who can make a small difference in the world. I don't need to cure cancer, but some small contribution to the world would be nice. I begin to make a mental list of the things that I already do to help make the world a better place. However, in addition to listing the good, I find myself listing the other things that counteract my feeble attempts.

I am diligent about recycling, but I've killed many trees by going through a roll or two of paper towels each day. I subscribe to a few newspapers and magazines only to recycle them unopened and unread. I contribute to certain charities, but, I must confess, I take the pens and pennies and use the greeting cards from other charities without sending them a contribution. In an effort to conserve gas, I map out an efficient route to run my errands, but I drive an SUV that seats seven to run said errands, when I only have one child. I buy organic fruits and vegetables but use pesticides on my lawn. I save leftovers but end up throwing them out a few days later. I don't wear fur, but I do wear leather. I don't check off the box on my license to donate my organs. I am still not sure where I stand on the disposal of my body after I die. I can't decide if I should take up more space on the earth that could be put to better use or if I should contribute to the greenhouse gases if I choose to be cremated.

Being confined affords ample opportunity to reflect upon everything and anything. As I watch the lightning rip through the sky, I can only hope that the shock of electricity I will receive in the morning will charge me in a positive way. May my electric dreams spider-vein out and send out a shockwave that will make a small difference in the world.

I WANT MY MOMMY!

CHAPTER XV

It's 10 p.m. The med closet opens for business one last time before we turn in. I ingest my pills, then open my mouth, and stick out my tongue as the nurse checks inside to make sure that I didn't "fake swallow." I do the hokey pokey patient shuffle and turn myself around, circling the Fishbowl a few times with my entourage, and then bid them good night. I hope the meds kick in quickly. Spending time in the Quiet Room is draining—not to mention all the calories I burned up by circling the unit. I make a mental note to request a pedometer from the staff in the morning.

As I enter my room, the light is off. Much to my dismay, Tess still lingers on. There she is, sitting in her bed with her back to me, the covers draped around her shoulders like a cape. I wouldn't dream of turning on the light. I must admit, I'm a bit afraid of her. I can see that she has a tiny light clipped onto her sketch pad. She does not acknowledge my presence and continues to dot away incessantly. I can tell she is in that obsessively creative mode.

Blindly, I search for my snowflake pajamas—yeah, that's right, you heard me, my snowflake pajamas. I'm not ashamed of them. I change in the bathroom, wash my face, brush my teeth, and then return to collapse onto the rigid mattress. The bed makes a squeaky fart-like sound.

"That wasn't me—it was the bed." I say defensively.

Of course, Tess does not respond.

While I lie there in the shadows, I take the opportunity to size up Tess the way she did to me earlier. The dim light illuminates her face and enables me to study it. On the surface, she is young. She looks to be about twenty-one, twenty-two years old. Her pearl-like skin is flawless, and the tiny diamond pierced through her nose shimmers incandescently. Her hair is light brown, short, and slicked back with the natural oils that come from not shampooing for a long period of time. I wonder... no...I need to know what her issues are. I need to get the upper hand in this relationship.

She intuitively senses me watching her and, without turning her head toward me, she says, "What the fuck are you looking at? Do you see something you like?"

"Uh, umm...no, nothing," I say nervously.

"Well, unless you're prepared to be my *beyotch*, quit looking at me!"

She says this in such a way that I'm not sure if she is joking or coming on to me.

"Oh God...I'm sorry! I didn't mean to...I mean, I don't want to be your...oh, never mind. Sorry!" I exclaim as I turn over and shrink back into the wall. So much for trying to get the upper hand.

My inner voice is now screaming, *I want my mommy! Lord, please don't let me be her beyotch! I don't want to be anybody's beyotch.* If my mother witnessed this, she would kick Tess into high, holy oblivion. My mom would never stand for such bullshit. I always admired my mother's strength. Why did she have to go and die on me?

I make a vow to myself that I am going to speak to the staff about this in the morning. Now they'll have to give me another room. For now, I lie there with one eye open. Thinking of my mother makes me ache deep down into the very core of my being. I miss her so. Sometimes she visits me in my dreams. The dreams contain no powerful message or revelation; we just sit casually at our old kitchen table, sipping coffee and chatting. My mom is very much alive and well in my dreams. Why did she have to leave this earth so soon? She was a gift to my sisters and me. I know it's cruel of me to say, but a part of me wishes that my father were taken instead of her. He wasn't making much of a contribution to society. Life is not fair. It makes no sense to me. Why take her?

During one of my mother's chemotherapy sessions, I confessed to her this very sentiment, and being a good Irish Catholic, she gasped.

"Shame on you, Janine! Don't you know that you can't barter with God? He takes who He takes, when, where, and how He chooses."

"Well, it's not fair. I'm mad at Him for choosing you so soon, and I'm mad at you for smoking all these years. Come on, Ma, everyone knows that smoking is a catalyst for lung cancer. Why? Why did you have to smoke?"

As she wiped the tears away from my eyes, she told me about the vices that had sustained her throughout her life.

"Coffee, cigarettes, and an occasional glass of red wine were all I had to relieve the stresses in my life. Everybody has to have something, right?"

"I guess, but did ya have to pick something that's bound to kill you?"

"Well, I like to live on the edge," she laughed.

She leaned over, kissed me on the cheek, and whispered into my ear, "You're my favorite, but don't tell your sisters. It's our little secret."

We giggled. When I was little, she used to whisper this to me every time we hugged. I kept our secret for quite some time, but later I learned that she whispered the same exact words to all of her daughters. This tradition continued into our adulthood.

We sat quietly for a few moments as I watched the IV bag full of cancer-fighting chemicals slowly drip into her vein. She stared out the window and smiled to herself.

"What? What is it?" I prodded.

She turned to me with a look of complete contentment and said, "I am a lucky woman. I have been truly blessed."

That's my mom. That statement sums her up completely. There she is, at fifty-six years of age, sitting in a hospital chair, ravaged with cancer, attached to an IV, and she considers herself a lucky woman.

"Is this what it comes down to? You're now channeling Lou Gehrig."

"No. Seriously, my life is complete. I have peace in knowing that I have done my job as a mother. I was able to raise my girls on my own and managed to keep a roof over our heads and food on the table. You see, God has always taken care of me. And now, well, now I'm just grateful that He didn't take me back then when you were young. So I can rest knowing that my girls will be okay." She held my hand as she went on. "I know you struggle with your bipolar condition, but I also know in my heart that you will be okay. I am truly proud of you. My daughters are the greatest gift that I have been given. Knowing that I have your love and your friendship is all a mother could ever ask for."

We held hands as tears continued to stream down my face. The TV was on in the background, set on PBS. The song from *Sesame Street* began to play, and my mom chimed in the way she did when I was a kid, singing, *"Sunny day, everything's A-okay. On my way to where the air is clean. Can you tell me how to get...how to get to Sesame Street...how to get to Sesame Street."*

A few weeks later, the phone rang just before midnight. It was Richard, my stepdad, calling to let me know that my mom had passed on. She suffered a heart attack brought on by the cancer, which had spread and surrounded her heart.

Now I completely understand. She was right. God did take care of her. He was kind enough to take her quickly, quietly, and with the least amount of suffering. She really was a lucky woman. She was truly blessed, and three little girls were truly blessed to be able to call her *Mom*. I guess that is all any daughter could ever ask for.

Drifting off to sleep in my hospital bed, I whisper to her, "Mom, you are *my* favorite. I love you and miss you. Come visit me tonight in my dreams and we'll sit, have some coffee, and we'll talk. Nighty night."

Helping Hands

CHAPTER XVI

Early the next morning, I wake up dead to the world. I am neither here nor there about what's about to happen to me in the ECT room. I feel no fear, no anticipation, no emotion—no hope, either.

Connie, the ECT nurse, enters my room to give me a shot to dry up all of my bodily fluids so I don't pee all over myself while under anesthesia. How thoughtful.

"Okay, Janine, just pull down your PJs for a moment so I can give you the shot."

I do as I'm told.

She swabs my butt with alcohol and sticks me. "There you go. The doctor will be in shortly to bring you to the ECT room. I'll see you in there."

I return to my bed and stare at the ceiling. It's not long before my mouth becomes parched as my saliva dries up. I try to pee but nothing comes out. A few moments later, my doctor enters the room.

"Good morning, Ms. Haynes," he says in his gentlemanly manner. "Are you ready to go to the treatment room?"

"As ready as I'll ever be," I respond.

I leave my room in my snowflake pajamas and walk alongside my doctor to the treatment room. My hair looks like a rat's nest, and I have one of the worst cases of morning breath I can remember. Being a proper gentleman, Dr. Kissilenko holds the door open and ushers me into the treatment room. It's a small room and sort of reminds me of a dentist's office. It even smells like one. I'm greeted by the nurse and the anesthesiologist.

In his soothing Bulgarian accent, my doctor guides me step-by-step.

"Okay, Ms. Haynes, please lie down on the bed while the nurse attaches the blood pressure cuff to your arm and the heart monitor to your chest."

The anesthesiologist approaches me with a clipboard full of questions.

"Did you have anything to eat or drink since midnight?"

"No."

"Any allergies?"

"I had an extreme reaction to an anti-nausea drug. I woke up vomiting violently after surgery once."

"Can you describe what happened?"

"Well, after they gave me the shot of the anti-nausea drug, I stopped vomiting, but I lost all control of my motor skills. I curled up in a ball and couldn't straighten out my limbs. My facial muscles were also affected. I looked like I had Bell's palsy. So, if possible, could you tweak the anesthesia just a little so I don't puke my guts up?"

"I think I can accommodate you," he says as he taps my arm in search of a good vein.

"Now, Ms. Haynes," Dr. Kissilenko continues, "I am going to swab your forehead and scalp so that I can attach the electrodes."

As he wipes my forehead, I ask if I can have a facial and seaweed wrap while I'm under. They chuckle slightly.

Then he brings over a mask attached to a small tank.

"This is a tank filled with oxygen. I am now going to put the mask over your nose and mouth, and I want you to take deep, slow breaths."

As he places the oxygen mask on me, my eyes fixate on the fluorescent light above. Maybe this is the only light I will ever see. When I overdosed, I never saw the white light that you're supposed to see when knocking on heaven's door. As I search for salvation on the hospital ceiling, my doctor interjects.

"Breathe in deep...breathe out...good. You are doing fine. Now we're going to administer the anesthesia. You will have a garlic-like taste in your mouth. Not to worry; that is only the anesthesia. Keep breathing deeply. You will be asleep shortly."

I thought I wasn't afraid, but as I drift off, a single tear is released. I reach out my hand for someone to hold, and, being the perfect gentleman that he is, Dr. Kissilenko holds my hand.

* * *

As I fade in and out of consciousness, I realize I've been moved to the Music Room. Despite the blanket I am swaddled in, my body shivers from the frigid air blowing down from vent in the ceiling.

I am greeted with, "Good morning, Starshine. The earth says hello! How are you feeling?"

"Where's your guitar?" I ask the tech sitting next to me. "I expected to be serenaded upon waking."

He just smiles warmly and replies, "Well if I did that for you, then I would have to do it for all the patients. Now we couldn't have that. But would you like some water? I can do that for you."

"Yes...please," I respond groggily as I zone out.

I wake up again still feeling woozy. Sitting up, I sip some water. In an attempt to preen myself, I rake my fingers through my hair, but they get stuck in a sticky, gel-like substance. My neck is sore and my jaw hurts. I feel like I've been pummeled.

"Good morning, again, Starshine. Do you want to get up and walk around?" the tech asks.

"I guess."

I stand up. My legs feel like jelly. I can't keep my balance so I reach out as he extends his hand, and I grab it. I lean on him as we walk to the blood pressure machine.

"Your pressure looks good. How about some breakfast?"

"Okay." I am famished.

He sits me down at a table in the Day Room and brings me a bagel and some orange juice.

"Can I get you anything else?"

"No thanks," I say. "By the way, the service is great here."

"I'm happy to hear that."

With a bit of confusion, I say, "I'm embarrassed. I know who you are, but I can't remember your name. I'm sorry."

"I'm Petey," he says as he puts his hand on my shoulder to comfort me. "Don't sweat it, Janine. It happens sometimes with the ECT."

I eat my bagel. Then Petey helps me to my room. I sleep most of the day away. Apparently one of the perks of having volts of electricity sent through your entire body is that the staff leaves you alone for the day. I don't have to attend any of the group sessions.

I need a shower badly. You know it's bad when you can actually smell yourself. I stagger to the bathroom and run the water in shower. In the ACU, the water never seems to get hot enough. My guess is that they don't want the patients to scald themselves. My knees feel weak so I sit down on the shower floor, close my eyes, and let it all wash away—the stickiness in my hair from the conductor gel, the bandage on my arm from the IV, the guilt over my actions, the sorrow from the repercussions—I let it all wash away.

I must have been in the shower for some time. It takes a long while to cleanse one's soul and give birth to a new beginning. Tess, however, isn't so patient. She bangs on the door repeatedly and then screams at me.

"Get out already!"

I don't answer her so she barges into the bathroom.

She sees me sitting on the shower floor. "What the fuck are you doing?" she asks with a hint of concern.

"Not much, just baptizing myself," I say nonchalantly.

She storms out, yelling, "Well, I have to take a shit!"

Little do I know, she goes to get one of the female health techs.

"Janine? Are you okay?" A tech opens the door a crack.

It is Eva, the same tech who I remember pushing down when she tried to help me out of the shower during my last visit. I remember it clearly, because when I pushed her, I didn't think she would slam into the wall and fall down. After all, she's about six feet tall and I'm only five two.

I remain seated in the shower as she enters the bathroom.

"I'm fine," I say. "I just needed a good wash."

"Well, it's time to come out now." She hands me a towel with one hand and extends the other hand to help me up. I reach out and she pulls me up, wraps my bathrobe around me, and helps me back to bed.

"I'm sorry," I say to her.

"For what?" she asks, perplexed.

"Don't you remember? During my last visit, I was so paranoid of everyone. I never meant to push you to the floor."

Eva looks at me with a crooked smile. "You never pushed me down, Janine. I never fell to the floor."

"But I remember...the last time I was here, you were helping me out of the shower, and I was scared of you, so I pushed you."

"No, that didn't happen. Just think about it; you could never knock me down. I mean, look at me and look at you. That's just not possible."

"You mean to tell me that all this time I felt guilty about something that never actually happened?"

"Nope...never happened. But if it had, I would have accepted your apology."

"Huh." I wonder what else in my life is imaginary.

Eva exits the room, leaving me with the dilemma of some other incidents that supposedly happened during that hospital visit. I remember meeting a girl who I grew up with. We were good friends. We went to school together, hung out together, and took gymnastics together. Even on our own time, we would do cartwheels, handstands, and flips right in the middle of the street. Although we were very close back then, we lost touch as childhood friends usually do. So when I saw her in the ACU, I did not recognize her.

She walked over to me. "Oh my God! Janine?" she asked. "It's me, Kate."

"Katie!" I exclaimed. We hugged and held hands for a moment. "What are you doing here?" I asked her.

I could tell she was embarrassed as she looked around and then whispered, "I'm in for alcohol. What about you? What are you here for?"

"I'm bipolar!" I boasted, as if being bipolar was somehow better than being an alcoholic.

That was about the extent of the conversation. At the time, I was flying so high in such a manic state that I was flipping out into another galaxy somewhere.

Later on that day, during deck time, I was flitting about like a little shutterbug doing twirls and casting love spells on everyone in my path. I happened to overhear Katie say to someone, "She won't even come over and talk to me. Why won't she talk to me?"

Aside from our initial conversation, for whatever reason, I was not capable of communicating verbally with Katie. So I decided to acknowledge her presence in my own unique way. In a way that only she would understand.

I shouted over to her, "Hey, Katie! This one's for you!"

Then I turned and did a cartwheel in her honor, hoping that it would spark a memory from our gymnastic days together. After my execution, Katie smiled at me with complete understanding. Our nonverbal bonding was momentary; I was escorted back to my room and reprimanded for my gymnastic display.

That was the last I saw of Katie. Looking back, I wish that I could have held her hand instead of just doing a cartwheel. I guess what it all came down to was my pride. I was just as embarrassed as she was to be committed to a psychiatric ward. When we were kids, neither one of us could have ever envisioned that our little world filled with backbends, flips, and cartwheels, would lead us tumbling into each other years later. I wish I could have spotted Katie the way I did when she practiced her back flip. In turn, when I fell down back then, she would hold out her hand and help me up.

The flips we did as kids were so much easier than the flips we do when we're all grown up. The tumbles of our childhood only bruised the body, not our soul, not our spirit. I only wish, during our hospital stay together, I could've lent her that helping hand. Unfortunately, at the time, I was doing my own grownup version of a back flip, and it never dawned on me to ask her to spot me as well.

Katie, if you happen to read this, *I hope you understand.*

Neenie-in-a-Bottle

CHAPTER XVII

My childhood nickname was Neen or Neenie and remains so today. I guess Neen was short for Janine and Neenie was the endearing version. Not surprisingly, I chose imaginative, pretend play for my pastime as opposed to my older sister, who played with more realistic, tangible objects like Barbie dolls. *I Dream of Jeannie* was my all-time favorite TV show with *Bewitched* trailing slightly behind. These shows intrigued me. How I longed to have such magical powers! As a child, I prayed every night for God to grant me such powers, and I promised Him that I would use those powers to perform good deeds. Unlike my television role models, Jeannie and Samantha, who only used their powers for menial tasks like cleaning up the house or turning someone into a mule, I would expand my horizons and use my powers for the greater good of humanity. Please don't be mistaken, I intended to use my powers for my own selfish pleasures, including making my bed and making sure that each night there would be strawberry licorice under my pillow. My greater plan, however, sounded more like a Miss America platform. I planned to use my magical powers to heal the sick, feed the hungry, and clothe the poor.

While I remained optimistic that God was going to grant me superpowers, I played the role of Jeannie for a good portion of my childhood. Like Jeannie, I would wear my long blonde hair in a high ponytail. Then I would raid my mother's scarf drawer and tuck the scarves into my hair and drape them around my face. I would also stick some scarves into my pink leotard so they would cascade down my legs and flow softly while doing a belly dance and singing the "da-dah-dah-dah-de-da-dah-dah-dah" tune from the opening of the show. It goes without saying that every genie has a bottle, and my life-size makeshift bottle was behind the black leather lounge chair in my living room. The caddy-cornered position of the chair created the perfect interior space for a genie bottle. The decorating philosophy for a genie bottle is *the more scarves and throw pillows, the better.* Needless to say, my mother's scarf drawer was emptied. The couch, along with every bed in the house, was stripped of any throw pillows that would be suitable for the décor of a genie bottle.

I have to say, my mother was unperturbed by it all. Even though she was scarf-less and pillow-less, she always encouraged my creative side. While other mothers might have been concerned that their child lived in a somewhat constant state of fantasy, mine just chalked it up to a vivid imagination. One year, my mom even sewed an authentic looking genie costume for Halloween, which I graciously donned year round—but only in the house, of course. Anything else would just be crazy...right?

In fifth grade, I decided to share this vivid part of my imagination with a girl named Amelia. She was one of the first African American girls to be bused to my school during the seventies integration program. Our class picture that year looked something like this: three tiers of children with very, very pale faces and a singular very, very tall, very, very dark-skinned girl with one very, very large afro standing smack in the middle of the top tier.

Amelia was my friend. She was different, yet I felt comfortable enough with her to let her in on my genie-like powers. At first, she was skeptical and asked to see my genie bottle. So I obliged. The next day, I brought in my genie bottle made from one of my mother's Chianti bottles. Remember those wine bottles, the kind made of green glass with woven straw around the bottom? In order to make the genie bottle genuine, I stuffed it with some cotton balls to represent throw cushions. Then I cut up tiny snips from my mother's pink scarf and stuck in a pair of stolen Barbie doll shoes from my sister's collection. After Amelia peered into the genie bottle, she became a believer.

Not everyone was so nice to Amelia. One day, one of the boys in my class called her a bad word, and she got really mad. This bad word sent the boy straight to the principal's office, and he was suspended from school for a few days. This bad word also made my teacher cry. When someone asked the teacher why she was crying, she said that she never thought hatred could be passed down. I didn't understand what she meant by this. So just before dinner, I asked my mom.

"Mom? What's a nigger?" I asked curiously.

"What!" she gasped.

"What's a nig—"

She put her hand over my mouth and stopped me midsentence. "Shush! I heard what you said. That's a bad word."

"Well, Robert called Amelia a nigger, and he had to go to the principal's office. What's a nigger, Mommy?" I naively questioned.

"Janine, stop saying *that word*! I don't want to hear you say *that word* again!" she exclaimed.

"Well, what does it mean? And why did Amelia get so mad? And why did it make my teacher cry?" I persisted.

She sat me down on one of the kitchen chairs, pushed aside the pile of unfolded laundry that was on top of the table, set down her coffee mug, and lit up a cigarette. She took one long, deep drag of her cigarette and slowly exhaled the smoke sideways through her lips so as not to blow the smoke in my direction.

"Listen, Janine, sometimes people call other people bad names. That's not nice. It hurts feelings. Calling a person with dark skin *that word* is not nice and hurts their feelings. Remember, you didn't like it when someone told you that you looked like a ghost because your skin is so pale. Right?"

I nodded.

"Now, you might hear other people using *that word*, but that doesn't make it right, and no one in this household is allowed to use *that word*. We are white people and they are black people, and I even read somewhere that sometimes black people like to be called..." she pauses then slowly enunciates each syllable, "*A-fro A-mer-icans.* Say it with me now."

"Ah-froo-Ah-mer-ee-cans," I repeated.

"Good!" she exclaimed. "Can you understand any of this, Janine?"

"I think so. It's not nice to call people names, but why do they call them black when they're really brown? And why do they call us white when we're really beige?"

My mother burst out into laughter and hugged me. "You're right! You're so observant. I guess whoever named the races must have been color blind."

"Mom, what races are you talking about? Running races? And, what does color blind mean?"

She caressed my cheek and sighed. "Well, let's just save that for another time."

This was how my single-parent, liberal-minded, bra-burning mother handled her first politically correct conversation with her fifth-grade daughter.

When I saw Amelia the next morning, I asked if her feelings were still hurt. She looked so sad and asked me to give her a magic potion that would make her skin light and her hair blonde like mine. She said that if I really was a genie and her friend, then I must help her. With my genie-ness at stake, I acquiesced. I told her that I would bring her the magic potion the next day.

At dismissal, I ran all the way home and waited impatiently for my mother to get home from work. I told her about my dilemma, and she completely understood. She helped me put together a magic potion made up of one part baby powder and one part golden glitter. She put the concoction into a little baggie with a twist tie. She also helped me to come up with some words to cast the magic spell.

It went something like this:

Magic dust, if you may, if you might,
grant Amelia's wish tonight.
Turn her dark skin to light.
If she does not turn light by tonight,
then she will know that her dark skin is alright.
For not even magic dust can change what is outta sight!

I rehearsed this over and over again on my way to school. We met in one corner of the schoolyard where I recited the spell. Amelia towered over me, so I had to have her bend down to sprinkle the magic dust onto her shoulders and into her enormous afro. After the spell was cast, we stood in line to go into school.

During class, some of the girls kept telling Amelia how pretty the golden glitter looked in her hair. I noticed that she looked happy again and even smiled a few times. At dismissal, before Amelia got on the mysterious school bus that always returned her back to her neighborhood far, far away, she walked over to me and asked me to undo the spell. She decided that she was fine just the way she was.

I was happy for Amelia. Most of all, I was relieved that I didn't have to reveal to her that I was a mere mortal just like her and did not possess any superpowers. Amelia came to that realization on her own when I fell flat on my face when she tried to teach me how to jump rope, double-Dutch style. My genie jig was up, but our friendship continued.

A wealth of wisdom came along with that experience. With my mother's help, I was able to see that even though I was not Jeannie, I was a genie in my own right. My mother told me that my name meant *gracious gift*. She told me that I have the gift of compassion and that compassion is more powerful than any magical spell that Jeannie could ever conjure up. I also learned that our words and our actions are far more powerful. Through our words and actions, we mortals have the capability to either help or hurt each other.

With this newfound wisdom, I put the cork on my genie bottle and placed it on a shelf in my room. Every now and then, I would open it up to let the Neenie-in-a-bottle out, but I had decided to put my newfound gift of compassion to use in a more practical way. Fat Linda was my next subject. I tried to help her lose weight in order to lose the title "Fat" that always preceded her name. I became her fitness trainer and dietitian. I would pass her notes in class and tell her to meet me after school. We would run around the block a few times with the hope of putting an end to the torture she endured when the kids pulled her pants down just for a laugh. When the ice cream truck came around, I was there to help her to say no to that second Good Humor bar. My act of compassion was small, but the intention was great. Although Linda never lost any weight, she gained a friend in her ostracized world that was her childhood.

Who says that too much television is not good for you? *I Dream of Jeannie* fostered my vivid imagination, which sparked a belief that I had the power to do anything. I learned to use my special powers in a more realistic, yet still magical, way.

Thanks, Jeannie!

Hope

CHAPTER XVIII

Forgive me for jumping back and forth between my past and present. I tend to occupy my mind in that way whenever I'm in the hospital.

For the most part, the rest of my stay consists of a series of shock treatments and group therapy sessions. Over the next couple of weeks, I watch as other patients come and go, and wonder when it will be my turn. Fortunately, Tess and I go our separate ways when they move me into Margaret's old room at the end of the hallway. I never see Tess again, but remnants of her existence still remain.

After about a week of enjoying my solitude, Petey stops by my room.

"Hey, Janine, you left this in your old room." He hands me a piece of paper.

It is a portrait of me drawn in a million little dots, reminiscent of Tess's work.

"That's really cool, Janine," Petey says. "I didn't know you could draw like that."

"I didn't do this; Tess did," I state.

"Tess? Who's Tess?" he asks.

"My old roommate," I replied. "Don't you remember?"

I can tell from the look on his Petey's face that he is concerned.

"You didn't have a roommate," he replies.

"Yes, I did. We shared the semi-private room by the Fishbowl."

"Yeah, you were in the semi-private room, but you didn't have a roommate."

I stop right there in my tracks, knowing that if I insist further it will only extend my hospital visit. The best thing to do is to turn this conversation into a joke.

"Just kidding, Petey…gotcha…psych!" I recover quite nicely. "I know I didn't have a roommate, silly. I drew it. I have a background in art. This kind of dotting is called pointillism. I learned it in college."

"Oh, you got me good!" he says, relieved. "I was scared that they might have to up your antipsychotic medication."

We laugh as he leaves the room, and I swiftly retreat to the bathroom with drawing in hand, close the door, and sit in repose on the toilet to pee. I study the portrait. It is a fine piece of artwork. Such detail…such an accurate likeness. I should be proud. It should be framed for all to admire. Instead, I bring it over to the sink and watch as the water from the faucet runs over it and bleeds the million little dots into one. Then I tear it into tiny pieces and flush it down the toilet along with my urine. The girl who only existed in the shadows of my guilt-ridden mind is gone with one flush. The evidence of my psychosis—destroyed.

My nineteen-day stint at the ACU comes to a close, and I am released with the agreement that I will continue ECT on an outpatient basis. My treatments last for the next nine months, and the dense fog of my depression slowly begins to lift; I am able to see some blue sky peeking through. Hope is reaching out to me for the first time in a long while, and I am ready to embrace it.

Hope can be like an illusive magic trick. It's a *now you see it, now you don't* kind of thing. Just like in a magic show, we can either allow ourselves to be wowed by it or skeptical of it. With hope comes the belief that things can and will get better. Hope gives us the motivation to go on even during the most trying times in our lives. Without hope, we can only exist on a substandard level of being. When hope is lost, so is the spirit.

Of course, now that I'm feeling better, it's easy to be Oprah-istic about it all. That's just it. When you have hope, it's like finding that old comfy sweater that has been in the back of your closet for an eternity. Once you put it back on, you wonder why you ever took it off.

I wish, at this point in my story, I could impart to you the secrets for attaining and maintaining a state of well-being, but we all know that's impossible. It's different for all of us. There are too many variables in life to have one specific formula. If only we could remember somehow, some way, when we are in the depths of our own despair, that hope is hiding somewhere in the back of our messy closet, waiting to be found and donned once again. And, if for some reason you can't find it, by all means, go out and get a new one.

The point is, never give up on hope...*never.*

The Purple Bracelet

CHAPTER XIX

From the comfort of my home, I watch as the seasons come and go—all the while receiving ECT. At first, the treatments are once a week, then once every two weeks, and finally once a month. It's not until nine months later, January of the following year, that my doctor and I decide I am ready to phase out ECT altogether and just continue with my medication regimen. At this point, because of the excessive shock treatments, a good portion of my short-term memory has been erased, and so has a fair amount of my long-term memory. My sense of direction is obliterated. I get lost driving to places that I've been to a thousand times before. Names of people escape me, and not just mere acquaintances. Yet, my childhood memories remain vivid.

In my opinion, though, the memory loss is a small price to pay for getting my sanity back. It appears that the ECT erased bits and pieces of the last ten to fifteen years of my life. I fill in the blanks by sifting through family photos and asking my husband a string of questions about family occasions and vacations.

I do, however, remember that this is the morning of my last shock treatment. I wake up feeling like it's a national holiday. So, I decide to dress up for the occasion. I carefully plan my outfit. It's an upward progression of symbolic colors: I start with black boots to represent the darkness of depression. Then I choose a pair of gray pinstripe slacks to show the lengthy haze of my illness. In honor of the homeless woman who imparted her lore of green being the color of insanity, I wrap myself in my familiar, comfortable, green sweater. Then in her memory, I slip on the purple bracelet she gave me years ago, the very bracelet she said was once green and turned to the healing color of purple. Wearing it gives me the mystical sense of all things coming full circle. Just like the homeless woman moved on from that street corner, I am moving onward.

As I enter the ACU in anticipation of my last shock treatment, I am welcomed by some of the staff.

"Janine, you look great!" Connie, the ECT nurse says. We've come to know each other over the past nine months. People who choose to go into this particular field of healthcare are truly a godsend to individuals like me. I am so grateful to all of them. I hope they know their efforts are not in vain.

I graciously sit down in one of the chairs outside the Fishbowl and wait patiently for my last treatment. While I wait, a few patients pass me by on their walk around the Circle. Some make eye contact with me. I just smile. Then after a second trip around the Circle, some patients stop to talk to me.

One man sits down beside me and says that he has found a way to break out of the mold that society forces upon us. He proceeds to share his pearls of wisdom.

"Ya know what I do to beat the system?" he asks me.

I humor him. "What? Tell me."

"First, I sprinkle the pepper on my food before I sprinkle on the salt. You see how that changes things? Even when you're in a restaurant, the waiter always asks if you want salt and pepper. It's never pepper and salt. Well, I'm changing all of that."

"Wow, that's interesting!" I respond. "Thanks for the tip. I'll try it out."

As he walks away, he tells me, "Pass it on. Get the word out there."

"I'll do my best."

Two other women who are on their second trip around the Circle also stop to talk to me.

"I like your boots," one of them says.

"Thanks."

"Are you a doctor?" the other one asks.

"No. I'm an outpatient," I say. "I'm here for ECT."

"What's that?"

"Shock treatment," I translate, knowing they will understand this term.

One of them is quick to react. "Really?" she says incredulously. "But you don't look crazy. I'm sorry...I didn't mean that you're... I just think that you look so normal, dressed up and all."

"Thanks for the compliment," I say, wondering if it really is a compliment. "I guess this is what *my kind of crazy* looks like at its best."

One of them laughs, but the other is quick to defend her sanity. "Well, I'm not crazy. I'm just addicted to heroin. I put in for my seventy-two-hour release, and then I'm rid of this place."

I say nothing to her; I can tell that she just isn't ready to face her addiction. She walks away, cursing under her breath about how other facilities are much nicer than this one. The other woman stays behind and sits down next to me.

"You know, my doctor wants me to get shocked, too. What's it like?" she inquires.

For a brief moment in time, I am the doctor and she is my patient as I explain the ins and outs of ECT. She listens closely to my opinion of the pros and cons. I can see from her dreary appearance that she is caught up in that all-too-familiar riptide and is being dragged under.

After our conversation, she thanks me for the information and reaches out her hand. As I hold her hand, she spots the purple bracelet.

"That is so pretty," she sweetly comments.

With that, I realize what needs to be done. I slip off the purple bracelet and give it to her.

"Take it," I say. "It was given to me by an old woman who told me the bracelet helped her to heal. Wear it until you get well, then pass it on to someone else."

In awe, she holds the shimmering purple bracelet up to light, and, in turn, I am able to witness the awesome sparkle of hope in her eyes. This small gesture has brought a smile to her face, warmed my heart, and touched my soul deep down to very core of what it is that makes us human.

The Gift

CHAPTER XX

As I write this last chapter, tomorrow will be two years exactly to the day when I attempted to take my life. How fitting it is to sit here and reflect on such a dismal period in my life. Things would have turned out differently had I been successful in my attempt. Instead of being six feet under, I am privileged to observe the snowflakes accumulating on the ground, forming a crystallized bond upon the earth.

It also happens to be a snow day for my son. We sit together in our little den, each at our separate keyboards, finishing off this story. I have yet to read his ending to the chapter that he started at the beginning of this book. The ECT may have erased some of my memory leading up to my suicide attempt, but it hasn't for my son. He can still describe in great detail the events from that horrific night. I wait with anticipation as he feverishly types away. I pray that he has come to a place of healing, forgiveness, and some sort of resolution. It would be the greatest gift he could bestow upon me.

As I sit here typing from my perspective, the entire experience has allowed me to look at the world as if I were looking at it for the first time. In addition to the ECT wiping out some of my memory, interestingly, it also erased part of my sensory perception. So, in essence, the treatments have allowed me to freshly view the world all over again. For the last two years, the sun has been brighter, the trees have been greener, and the stars seem to sparkle in high definition. I admire a house in my neighborhood that I've never seen before, though my husband reminds me that it's always been there. What's more is that the people in my life are even more real, more tangible, and more available to me than ever before. The freckles peppered on my son's face tickle me with delight. When I hold my husband's hand, it's even warmer and more quilted than I remember. By the graces from the powers that be, I have been spared from death by my own hand. To sum it up best, my life is a do-over. I have gone through a metamorphosis that can only be described as a phenomenal rebirth.

I can't help but think about the Raven and the Turtle. One day while I was rearranging my bookshelves, the black feather that the Raven gave to me came floating out from one of the books I had with me during my last hospital stay. It landed gently on the floor, and the Raven's words came flooding back to me. She was right; I am the Turtle. I have gone within my shell. Over these last two years, I have meditated and, to some degree, I have healed. I must confess, despite the risk of being hospitalized again, that in a sense I am also Mother Nature. I have been returned to this good earth to tend to it, to my family, and most of all, to myself. I have been given a gift that was wrapped up and delivered to me in the form of *my kind of crazy.* The grueling experience of being bipolar has forced me to grasp that Holy Grail that I've been searching for. I see it now, right there in front of me. For me, that Holy Grail is the wealth of knowledge and wisdom bestowed upon me through the journey into the dark places of my soul, only to be returned to the light once again.

That being said, I present to you my special gift—it is the gift of being crazy. Through the years, there were times when I felt so ashamed of that label; but now I understand that being crazy is something I must embrace. I have no other choice. After living with bipolar disorder all of these years, I've come to believe that it's not at all a disorder but, rather, a human condition that has taught me so many life lessons. In turn, I have been able to accept the gift of the purple bracelet—the gift of healing.

So, if you happen to be one of the 5.7 million Americans who struggle with a mental illness, please know that you are not alone. The truth is we are all a little crazy in one way or another. Although my case is more severe than most, those dealing with a mental illness suffer in silence due to the stigma attached to the diagnosis. It is my hope that, like a jagged lightning bolt in a storm, my own tumultuous storm can send a positive jolt to help even just one other person. Then, this crazy journey of mine has been a worthwhile one.

All I ask in return is what the old woman who gave me the purple bracelet asked of me—*pass it on.*

P.S.: Steven's Chapter Conclusion

CHAPTER XXI

I just received my son's conclusion to the chapter he began writing earlier in my story. Below is the gift that he has given to me.

Every March, my behavior seems to change. March happens to be the month that my mother tried to kill herself. As it gets closer and closer to the anniversary date, I become quieter, lose my sense of humor, and can't sleep at night. Today is a snow day and school is closed. My mom asked me to finish up my chapter.

I am beginning to feel a little less uncomfortable around the topic of suicide. Personally, I never thought that we would all be standing tall right now. I thought it would just be my dad and me, but I was wrong. My mom seems to be fine, and my life has continued. I have made major improvements. My focus turns to entering high school. In high school, I will be faced with issues regarding alcohol and drugs, but a part of me remembers that I have been through a lot worse. I know I am mentally strong enough to handle the peer pressure and do the right thing. I am stronger because of my mother.

I am almost fourteen now and have a lot going on in my life. Between friends, school, and sports, I have very little time to myself; but I am aware that I am one of the lucky ones compared to those who live in Darfur or even New Orleans. Their lives have been destroyed, their homes are gone, and for many, their families are gone, too. Yet somehow I feel connected to them. It makes me feel like I need to help out.

For example, on Fridays when I go into town with my friends after school, after spending some money on junk food, I usually have change left over. During the holiday season, there is always a Salvation Army man ringing a bell outside the door to one of the stores. I pull the change out of my pocket and place it in the bright red canister, knowing that it will help someone at some point—someone whose life has been picked apart and destroyed.

Living through the ordeal of my mother's suicide attempt has affected me in many ways, some good and some bad. Sometimes I get flashbacks of that night. In another way, though, her illness has made me a stronger person and more sensitive than before, because I have seen the worst and so I cherish the good when it's around. My parents remind me how brave I was in a situation where I could have just screamed in a corner somewhere, but instead I called my neighbors and 911.

Recently, one night when I started to worry about the two-year anniversary coming up, my dad helped me to look at all of this in a better light. He said that although the incident was a terrible thing to endure, in a way it changed all of our lives for the better. My mom decided to get ECT, which she was always so afraid of getting in the past. Now that she has been properly treated, I have my mother back. All of her is back. My dad said that we can choose to acknowledge the end result, which was a positive one. A new day really has begun. Instead of visiting my mother's grave on this second anniversary of her suicide attempt, I'm going outside to snow tube down my driveway with my friend, Jared! See ya!

Steven Haynes, survivor

Pass It On

If you would like to order
a symbolic purple bracelet,
like the one mentioned in my story,
please contact:

Leaaron Designs

www.ddince@mac.com

Special Thanks

I will attempt to utter the names of friends and family who have read my pages as I fed them my story, chapter by chapter. No doubt, I will leave someone out. Please forgive me, in advance, for any oversights. Your loving words of encouragement helped bring my story to its fruition. I am eternally grateful.

To Linda Crowley-Zimmer, my sweet little sister, my eternal shadow, your playful, carefree ways will follow me all the days of my life.

To Kathleen Crowley-Carucci, my Irish twin, thank you for steering me in the right direction and reining me in during my wild years, which was not always an easy task.

To my stepdad, Richard Young, I am eternally grateful to you for lovingly caring for my mother during the last months of her losing battle with lung cancer, while simultaneously fighting your own personal battle with cancer. You are as strong as piano wire.

To Janet and Jerry Haynes, I thank you for taking care of me as if I were your own daughter. Janet, I want to thank you for taking the time to read my manuscript. Even though you cried the entire time, I am moved by your love and concern.

To Ondrea Haubner, you are my favorite sister-in-law. I've always wanted to come back as your child. Aly (Albo) and Danielle (LuLu) are very, very lucky.

To Jeanine Anaya, this book happens to be the end product of your gentle coaxing. I cherish our special relationship and your willingness to follow me whenever I go off on a meandering tangent.

To Laurie Hamburg, your friendship is unwavering. You were always there for me, as well as for my family, during those dark times. Thank you for lending me your writer's savvy.

My thanks extend to the rest of the Hamburg family, Steve, Rebecca, and Jared. There is no doubting your true friendship.

To John Carucci, I thank you for your professional tidbits. I appreciate your creative nature and cherish the early years when life was a blank canvas. You will always hold a special place in my heart.

To Jillian Carucci and Anthony Carucci, may life be kind to you both, and may you never stop dreaming.

Thanks to my outta-boro girls, Lisa Eberlein, Donna Busch, Michele Grisafi, Karen Taverone, and Chris Cutrona, for being eager to read my manuscript and all of my essays.

To the therapy-by-email members, Donna Nilsen (No. 1 fan), Cindy Downes, Laura Fasciglione, Joan Roe, Cathy Rossi, MaryJean Schaeffer, Annmarie Constantino, and Michelle Kopicki. I thank all of you for including me in your circle and for giving me such great feedback.

My love goes out to two very important women in my life and my son's life, Debbie Sturdivant and Nadia Willoughby, who helped take care of my son when I was not able. Words cannot describe my gratitude, and I know both of you hold a special place in Steven's heart as well.

To Chris Hikawa, I am grateful for your friendship, and I thank you for looking over some initial contracts.

To Regina Kay, thanks for always being in my corner.

To Friday nights with Andrea Papa, Dana Dince, and Maria Larramendi, thank you for the laughter—it's much more effective than any pill in my medication regimen.

To Laurie Fessler Friedmann, thanks for finding those eleventh-hour glitches. You are a gentle soul.

Thanks to the O'Keefe tribe, Kevin, Donald, Lynne, Cori, Kailee, and Sterling, for taking the time to read my manuscript. Kevin, you've been more like a brother to me than an uncle. I always look forward to our time together. Donald, you are a kindhearted soul—never forget that.

To my nana-gram, Catherine, the matriarch of the O'Keefe tribe, all my love I give to you.

And, finally, I want to thank my father, Robert Crowley. Strangely enough, your absence in my life has taught me much about myself, my illness and life in general. I know you struggle with your own issues, but you must know that I am grateful for the lessons I've learned, both in your presence as well as in your absence. I am who I am because of it. I will forever be your little snowflake.

About and Not About the Author

Janine Crowley Haynes is not a doctor. She is certainly not a celebrity who can use her illness as a platform, and she is in no way, by any stretch of the imagination, a prize-winning author.

What she is, however, is an expert on being crazy—over thirteen years of personal experience. Janine is not alone with her illness, she is only one in 5.7 million adult Americans diagnosed with a mental illness in a given year. She decided to share her story of living with bipolar disorder with the hope of dismantling the stigma, shame, and isolation that one with a similar illness might experience.

It is her belief that one must embrace their inner-craziness in order to heal, evolve, and move forward to help change the societal perception of mental illness. Not unlike diabetes, mental illness should be understood on a biochemical level—not be viewed as a character flaw. When the brain gets sick, it exhibits symptoms that need to be addressed and managed just like any other physical ailment.

6033876R0

Made in the USA
Lexington, KY
10 July 2010